Sandwiches, Panini, and Wraps

QUARRY

Sandwiches, Panini, and Wraps

Recipes for the "Anytime, Anywhere" Meal

Dwayne Ridgaway

QUARRY BOOKS

First published in the United States of America by
Quarry Books, an imprint of
Quayside Publishing Group, Inc.
100 Cummings Center
Suite 406-L
Beverly, MA 01915-6101
Telephone: (978) 282-9590
Fax: (978) 283-2742
www.quarrybooks.com

Library of Congress Cataloging-in-Publication data available.

ISBN - 13: 978-1-59253-153-0
ISBN - 10: 1-59253-153-9

10 9 8 7 6 5 4 3

Design: Q2A Design
Cover Image: Allan Penn Photography

Printed in Singapore

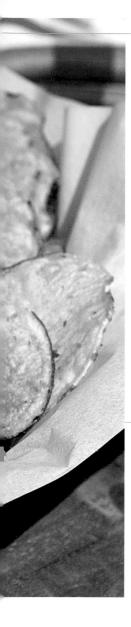

I have been given many opportunities in life for which I am very thankful. I dedicate this book to my loving parents, who have made many of those opportunities possible.

Thank you!

Contents

Introduction

People love sandwiches. And why not? A sandwich can be an entire meal, ready to go anywhere. From picnics to poolside, from a quick weekend lunch to a daily routine, sandwiches are the easiest, most portable meal there is. As increasingly more cafés and delis pop up on city streets and corners across the country, the popularity of the sandwich is at an all-time high. The variety is just as numerous as the places to find them—from wraps, clubs, and pitas to panini and more.

The sandwich was actually created by accident in 1762.

John Mantagu, the fourth Earl of Sandwich, was involved in a heated card game in which the stakes were high. He asked a servant to cook some meat and put it between two slices of bread so Montagu could eat his meal without geting his hands and cards dirty!

Sandwich history is a melting pot of cultural influence. Bread is found in some form or another in just about every culture, as are meat, vegetables, and cheese. Although it doesn't appear that one culture contributed more to sandwich history than another, it's clear by the number of Italian cold cuts available at any deli counter that Italy played a part in sandwich history. Panini, the latest trend in sandwich making, is also Italian for sandwich. In this country, Americans define panini as a grilled or pressed sandwich served warm, while an authentic Italian panini can be served hot or cold. In this book, I use the term *panini* to refer to grilled sandwiches.

While the ingredients of a panini can vary widely, the technique used to make one is one and the same. Start by piling a variety of succulent ingredients between two moist pieces of bread, oil or butter them, then press them between two hot grill plates, which toast the outside and melt the ingredients on the inside.

This book will cover much more than paninis, however. I plan to take you on a culinary journey that will not only please your palate but also offer exciting sandwich accompaniments, condiments, and serving suggestions. (I even snuck in several of my favorite recipes for portable desserts to serve with your sandwiches!)

I will also teach you some basics behind selecting bread, explore interesting and new sandwich ingredients, and introduce you to techniques and cooking equipment for easy sandwich building. With recipes for cold, hot, vegetarian, and salad sandwiches, there's something for everyone in this book. My recipes range from traditional to unique, and from simple to more involved, so beginner and experienced home cooks alike will find a sandwich to suit their skills and tastes.

chapter 1

Making a Great Sandwich Every Time

I don't think I've ever passed a sandwich shop window that didn't claim its sandwiches to be the "best," "award winning," "one and only," or "original." Truth be told, given the numerous ingredients available and the endless combinations that are possible, it's hard to imagine anyone being unable to make a good sandwich. With that said, however, there are some basic guidelines to keep in mind. First up: bread, without which a sandwich is not a sandwich.

[Bread]

Bread, in one form or another, is essential to making a great sandwich, whether it's sliced, flattened, wrapped, stuffed, or folded. Bread, as with all the ingredients, is a very personal choice. The qualities of breads range from firm, dense, airy, or hard to soft, thick, thin, white, wheat, sourdough, herbed, and more.

The basic rules to remember are as follows: Is the bread strong enough to hold the ingredients together? Is the bread dense enough to hold a sauce or oil? Is the bread large enough to accommodate the ingredients? Is the bread thin or thick enough, depending on the number of fillings? All of these are very basic points, but ones that can determine whether or not your sandwich is successful.

The flavor of the bread is as important as its size and shape. The bread should complement the inner ingredients. For example, a cinnamon raisin bread doesn't pair well with grilled tuna and wasabi mayonnaise, just as pumpernickle bread is probably too intense for everyday ham and cheese. When selecting the bread, keep in mind that all the flavors will have to work together.

FOR THE SPONGE:

1 teaspoon (4 g) dry yeast

1 cup (235 ml) warm water
(110°F to 115°F [approx. 45°C])

1½ cups (190 g)
all-purpose flour, sifted

FOR THE DOUGH:

1½ (6 g) teaspoons active
dry yeast

5 tablespoons (75 ml) warm milk

1 cup (235 ml) warm water
(110°F to 115°F [approx. 45°C])

1 tablespoon (15 ml) olive oil

3 cups (375 g)
all-purpose flour, divided

2 teaspoons (12 g) salt

Spray bottle filled with water

[To develop the sponge]
In the bowl of a heavy-duty mixer, combine yeast with the water. Gently stir and allow the yeast mixture to rest for 3 to 4 minutes, until foamy. Add the sifted flour to the yeast, stir to combine, then cover and let stand at room temperature for 12 hours.

[For the dough]
In a small bowl, add the yeast to the milk, and stir. Let stand for 3 to 4 minutes, until the mixture is foamy. Add the yeast-and-milk mixture, water, and olive oil to the sponge, and mix with a dough hook on medium speed. Add 2 cups (250 g) flour and the salt, and mix for 2 minutes at low speed. Increase to medium speed and mix for an additional 3 minutes, until the dough begins to pull away from the sides of the bowl. The dough should be firm enough to handle without sticking to the hands, but it should still very soft. Add the last of the flour slowly, mixing until well incorporated and the dough pulls away from the sides. Transfer dough to a clean, well-oiled mixing bowl. Turn the dough to coat it completely with oil. Cover the bowl with plastic wrap and set aside in a warm, draft-free spot. Let rise until tripled in size, about 45 minutes to an hour.

Transfer the dough to a floured work surface. For loaves: divide dough into four pieces, without punching down. Shape the dough into four 10" x 4" (25 x 10 cm) rectangles. Press down each loaf lightly with your fingers. For rolls: shape dough into rounds, each about 6" (15 cm) in diameter. Press down lightly with your fingers. For loaves and rolls: Cover the dough with a clean towel, and let rise in a warm, draft-free place for 90 minutes. (The dough will rise only slightly.)

Preheat oven with a baking stone to 400°F (200°C). Turn over the dough rectangles or rounds and transfer them to the hot baking stone, being careful not to deflate the dough. Bake for 25 to 30 minutes, until the bread just begins to turn golden. During the first 10 minutes of baking, spray the bread with the water bottle three times. Remove from oven; transfer bread to cooling rack.

[Makes 4 loaves (or 8 rolls)]

Ciabatta Bread

Ciabatta is an excellent choice for grilling sandwiches. The oil content and the rising process allow the loaf to triple in size during the first rising, creating air pockets throughout the loaf. Be patient—and let the yeast work its magic.

2½ cups (570 ml) warm water (105°F to 115°F [approx. 45°C])

1 tablespoon (12 g) active dry yeast

1 tablespoon (15 g) granulated sugar

7 cups (875 g) bread flour or all-purpose flour

1 tablespoon (18 g) salt

4 tablespoons (55 g) unsalted butter, softened

3 cups (705 ml) water

Combine yeast and sugar with ½ cup (120 ml) warm water in the bowl of a heavy-duty mixer, whisking to blend. Allow the mixture to rest until the yeast is foamy, about 5 minutes. With the dough hook on the mixer, add the remaining 2 cups (450 ml) water and about 3 ½ cups (440 g) flour to the yeast. Turn the mixer on and off a few times to gently incorporate the ingredients without tossing the flour out of the bowl. Mix on low speed, and add the remaining 3 ½ cups (440 g) of flour. Increase the mixer speed to medium, and beat, stopping to scrape down the bowl and hook as needed, until the dough comes together. If necessary, add a bit more flour, 1 tablespoon (8 g) at a time, until the dough comes together. Add the salt and continue to beat at medium speed, for about 10 minutes, until the dough is smooth and elastic. When the dough is thoroughly mixed, add the butter, 1 tablespoon (14 g) at a time, and beat until it is incorporated. If the dough separates with the addition of the butter, don't be alarmed—it will come back together with additional beating.

Turn the dough out onto a lightly floured work surface and shape into a ball. Place dough in a large, oiled bowl, and turn the dough to coat completely with oil. Cover with plastic wrap and place in a warm, draft-free place to rise until doubled in size, about 45 minutes to an hour.

Butter two 8 ½" × 4 ½" × 2¾" (21.5 × 11.5 × 7 cm) loaf pans and set them aside. Turn dough onto a lightly floured work surface—this should deflate the dough—and divide in half. Working with one half at a time, use your hands or a rolling pin to shape the dough into a large rectangle that measures about 9" × 12" (23 × 30.5 cm). Starting at the top, with a short side facing you, fold the dough about two-thirds of the way down the rectangle; then fold it again, so that the top edge meets the bottom edge. Pinch the seam to seal it. Turn the roll so that the seam is in the center, facing up, and turn the ends in just enough so that the roll will fit in the loaf pan. Pinch the seams to seal, then turn the loaf over so the seam is on the bottom again. Using the palms of your hands, plump the loaf to get an even shape. Place the dough into the pan, seam side down. Repeat this process with the second half of the dough. Cover the loaf pans with oiled plastic wrap and place in a warm, draft-free spot to rise, until doubled in size, about 45 minutes.

Meanwhile, center a rack in the oven, and preheat to 375°F (190°C). Bring 3 cups (705 ml) of water to a boil. Place water in a shallow, oven-proof baking pan, on the bottom rack of the oven. The steam released during baking will create a crisp crust. When the loaves have risen fully (test by poking a finger gently into the dough; the impression should remain), remove plastic wrap, and transfer loaf pans to the oven. Bake for 35 to 45 minutes, or until they are honey-brown in color, and an instant-read thermometer registers 200°F (95°C) when inserted deep into the center of a loaf. (Turn the dough out, and insert the thermometer from the bottom.)

If you'd like your loaves to be evenly brown, turn them out of the pans and bake them directly on the rack of the oven for the last 10 minutes of baking time. Otherwise, remove the loaves from their pans as soon as they come from the oven, and cool the breads on a rack. The loaves should not be cut until they are almost completely cool. Once completely cool, they can be stored in a brown paper bag for up to two days, or be frozen in airtight bags for up to one month. Thaw at room temperature before using.

[Makes 2 large loaves]

Classic White Loaves

This recipe-box staple bakes to a beautiful, round-top loaf that is perfect for toasting and large sandwiches.

Cracked Wheat and Honey Bread

The combination of multigrain flours and seeds delivers a hearty, country-style bread with a bit of sweetness from the added honey.

½ cup (50 g) fine cracked wheat

1½ cups (355 ml) boiling water

1 package active dry yeast (approx. 9 g)

⅓ cup (80 ml) warm water (110°F to 115°F [approx. 45°C])

4 tablespoons (55 g) softened butter or shortening

1½ tablespoons (27 g) salt

2 tablespoons (40 g) molasses

2 tablespoons (40 g) honey

1 cup (235 ml) milk

1 cup (125 g) whole-wheat flour

4 cups (500 g) all-purpose flour

3 tablespoons (15 g) flax seeds

3 tablespoons (15 g) pumpkin seeds, shelled and salted

1 tablespoon (15 g) poppy seeds

Place the cracked wheat in the boiling water, and cook for about 10 minutes, stirring occasionally to prevent sticking, until all the water is absorbed. In a large mixing bowl, dissolve the yeast with ⅓ cup (80 ml) warm water. Set aside to proof, about 5 minutes. Stir the butter, salt, molasses, honey, and milk into the cooked cracked wheat. Let cool until the mixture is lukewarm, and add to the yeast mixture. In a separate mixing bowl, use a whisk to combine the flours, flax seeds, pumpkin seeds, and poppy seeds. Add the flour mixture to the yeast mixture, 1 cup (125 g) at a time, stirring with a large spoon until the dough becomes stiff. Turn dough out onto a floured work surface and knead until smooth and elastic, about 10 to 12 minutes. Shape into a ball, and place in a buttered bowl. Turn dough to coat with butter, cover the bowl with plastic wrap, and set aside in a warm, draft-free spot to rise until doubled in size, about 1 to 1½ hours.

Preheat oven to 375°F (190°C). Punch down dough, divide it in half, and shape into two loaves. Place dough in well-buttered 9" × 5" × 3" (23 × 12 × 8 cm) loaf pans, cover with plastic wrap, and let rise again until doubled in size, or until the dough reaches the tops of the loaf pans. Bake for 30 to 35 minutes, or until the loaves sound hallow when tapped on top and bottom. Cool completely on racks.

1 package active dry yeast (approx. 9 g)

1 teaspoon (5 g) sugar

1½ cups (355 ml) warm water

1 teaspoon (6 g) salt

2 cups (250 g) whole-wheat flour

1½ cups (190 g) unbleached all-purpose flour

1 teaspoon (5 ml) olive oil

[Makes 8 pitas]

Pita Bread

The unique baking method for pita, paired with the yeast in the dough, causes the flat discs to rise and then puff, creating the bread's characteristic pouch. Pita dough can take on many variations; this particular recipe combines whole-wheat and all-purpose flour for a simple, flavorful sandwich bread.

In the bowl of a heavy-duty electric mixer fitted with the dough hook, combine the yeast, sugar, and warm water. Stir to blend. Let rest for about 5 minutes, until the yeast becomes foamy. In a separate mixing bowl, combine the salt with the whole-wheat and all-purpose flours. Whisk to combine. To the yeast mixture, add 1½ cups (190 g) of the flour mixture, turning the mixer on and off to incorporate the flour without tossing flour around the kitchen. Once combined, run the mixer on low and add the remaining flour, ½ cup (60 g) at a time, until all the flour is incorporated, and the dough gathers into a ball, about 5 minutes. Turn the dough onto a lightly floured work surface and knead until the dough is smooth and elastic, about 10 minutes. Transfer dough to a lightly oiled bowl and turn so the dough is coated with oil. Cover with plastic wrap, place in a warm, draft-free area, and let rise until doubled in size, about 1½ hours.

Preheat the oven, with a large pizza stone on the lower rack, to 500°F (260°C). Punch down the dough. Divide it into eight equal portions, and roll each piece into a ball between the palms of your hands. (Keep all pieces lightly floured and covered while you work.) Allow the balls of dough to rest, covered, on a lightly floured work surface for about 15 minutes. Using a floured rolling pin, roll each dough ball into an 8" (20 cm) circle, about ¼" (5 mm) thick. Make sure the circle is perfectly smooth— creases or seams in the dough can prevent the pitas from puffing up properly. Cover the disks as you roll them out, but do not stack them.

Place two pita rounds at a time on the hot pizza stone and bake for 3 to 4 minutes, or until the bread puffs up like a balloon, and is light golden in color. The pita rounds will bake quickly; be careful not to burn them. (Oven temperatures vary, causing cooking times to vary, as well. Be vigilant.) Remove the pitas from the oven and set on a rack to cool for 5 minutes. They will deflate, leaving a pocket in the center.

Wrap the pitas in a large kitchen towel to keep them soft; use as desired or store in a brown paper bag at room temperature for a few days. The pitas can be frozen in airtight bags or containers for up to one month. Thaw at room temperature before using.

Hard Sandwich Rolls

The trick to making good hard rolls at home is to use the steaming method during baking. Follow the directions closely to achieve the best hard roll. Poppy seed and onion variations are listed at right. Experiment, if you wish, with your own version. This recipe was adapted from Nick Malgieri's *How to Bake*.

FOR THE SPONGE:

1 cup (235 ml) warm water
(110°F to 115°F [approx. 45°C])

1/2 teaspoon (9 g) active dry yeast

1 1/2 cups (190 g) unbleached
all-purpose flour

FOR THE DOUGH:

1 1/4 to 1 1/2 cups (155–190 g)
unbleached all-purpose flour

1 1/2 teaspoons (9 g) salt

1 teaspoon (5 g) sugar

1 egg white, lightly beaten

Cornmeal for dusting

[To develop the sponge]

Place the water in a mixing bowl and sprinkle with the yeast. Add the flour and stir with a rubber spatula to produce a heavy paste. Cover the bowl and let the sponge rise at room temperature until the sponge has doubled in size, about 1 hour. Refrigerate overnight, or for at least 8 hours.

[For the dough]

Remove the sponge from the refrigerator and stir in 1 1/4 cups (155 g) of the flour, salt, sugar, and egg white. Knead by hand to form a smooth, elastic, and slightly sticky dough, about 5 minutes. Add more flour, 1 tablespoon (8 g) at a time, if the dough is too soft. Transfer the dough to an oiled bowl, and turn the dough to coat it with oil. Cover the bowl with plastic wrap and allow the dough to rise in a warm, draft-free spot until doubled in size, about 1 hour.

Turn the dough out onto a lightly floured surface and punch down. Divide the dough into 16 equal pieces. Working with one piece at a time, form each section into a small round by rolling in the palm of your hands. (Keep the remaining pieces loosely covered with plastic wrap.) Cover the rounds with a towel, and let rest for 5 minutes.

Stretch each round into a rough rectangle. Fold in the short ends to meet at the center, then roll up the long edge to form a tight cylinder. Place roll on a baking pan sprinkled with cornmeal, leaving enough room between rolls to allow them to double in size. Cover with oiled plastic wrap and let rise at room temperature until doubled in size, about 1 hour. When the rolls are almost doubled, prepare the oven for baking. Set racks at the middle and lowest levels of the oven, and preheat to 500°F (260°C). On the lowest rack, set a wide shallow pan to hold water.

When the rolls have risen, cut a deep slash, at an angle, the length of each roll. Open the oven and quickly pour a cup of hot water onto the hot pan. Close the oven for a minute, then open it again and place the rolls in the oven, being careful to avert your face from the steam that will billow out. Lower the open temperature to 450°F (230°C). After 10 minutes of baking, add another 1/2 cup (120 ml) of water to the pan. After 20 minutes, remove the water pan and lower the temperature to 350°F (175°C). Continue baking for 10 minutes longer, until the rolls are well browned and firm, with an internal temperature of 210°F (100°C) degrees. Remove from oven and cool on racks.

poppy seed rolls

FOR EGG WASH

1 egg

salt

1 teaspoon (5 ml) water

poppy seeds (about ½ cup [20 g])

Combine egg, salt, and water in a shallow bowl. Dip the tops of rounded, unbaked rolls into the egg wash, then dip the top into the poppy seeds, coating evenly. Place the rolls right side up on baking pan and cover to rise. Proceed to second rising without slashing the tops.

onion rolls

1 tablespoon (14 g) butter

small onion, finely chopped

sugar (about 2 teaspoons [18 g])

egg wash (see poppy seed variation, left)

Over medium-high heat, melt butter in a sauté pan. Sauté chopped onion until tender and beginning to brown. Sprinkle sugar over the onion, stir, and reduce heat to low and cook until caramelized, tender, and browned, about 15 minutes. Remove from heat. Prepare egg wash as directed at left for poppy seed rolls. Proceed with the wash directions, using cooled onions instead of poppy seeds to top each roll. Proceed to second rising without slashing the tops.

[Makes 2 long loaves]

French-Style Baguettes

It is not an easy task to create a French bread at home that rivals those from the bakery. French bread, highly prized for its distinctive crumb, crisp crust, and superb flavor, offers these characteristics as just reward for an exhaustive process. Here, I have adapted a recipe of James Beard's that he adapted from Julia Child.

1 ½ packages (14 g) active dry yeast

1 tablespoon (15 g) granulated sugar

2 cups (475 ml) warm water (100°F to 115°F [approx. 45°C])

1 tablespoon (18 g) salt

5 to 6 cups (625–750 g) all-purpose flour

3 tablespoons (27 g) coarse yellow cornmeal

1 tablespoon (15 ml) egg white, mixed with 1 tablespoon (15 ml) cold water

In a large bowl, combine the yeast with the sugar and warm water. Set aside until foamy, about 5 minutes. Mix the salt with the flour and add to the yeast mixture, 1 cup (125 g) at a time, stirring until a stiff dough forms. Transfer dough to a lightly floured work surface and knead until no longer sticky, about 10 minutes, adding additional flour as necessary. Shape the dough into a ball and place in a well-buttered bowl. Turn to coat evenly with butter, cover with plastic wrap, and place in warm, draft-free place to let rise until doubled in size, about 1½ to 2 hours.

Remove dough from bowl, punch down, and knead on a floured work surface for 10 minutes. Shape dough into a ball and return to the buttered bowl, again coating evenly with butter. When doubled in size (after about 1½ hours), remove dough from bowl and divide in half. Form two long loaves by rolling and stretching it between the palms of your hands. Place loaves on a baking sheet sprinkled with cornmeal. Cover with plastic wrap or a kitchen towel and let rise for 30 minutes. With a sharp knife create diagonal 1" (2.5 cm) slashes in the top of each loaf. Brush with egg white mixture. Place in a cold oven, and set temperature at 400°F (200°C). Bake until browned and hollow-sounding when tapped with the knuckles, about 35 minutes. Remove from oven and place on rack to cool.

2 packages active dry yeast (approx. 18 g)

1 cup (200 g) plus 1 teaspoon (5 g) granulated sugar

½ cup (120 ml) lukewarm water (90°F to 100°F [32°C-38°C])

1 stick (½ cup [112 g]) softened butter

½ cup (120 ml) warm milk

4 eggs, lightly beaten, divided

1 tablespoon (18 g) salt

4 to 4½ cups (500-560 g) all-purpose flour

In a large mixing bowl, combine the yeast with 1 teaspoon (5 g) sugar and warm water. Let rest until foamy, about 5 minutes. In another mixing bowl, whisk together the butter and the warm milk. Add the remaining 1 cup (200 g) sugar and blend well. Add butter, milk, and sugar mixture to the yeast mixture, and stir to combine. Lightly beat 3 of the eggs, add salt, combine, and add to the yeast mixture. Blend well. Add 4 cups (500 g) of flour, 1 cup (125 g) at a time, kneading with your hands in the bowl, to form a soft dough.

Turn the dough out onto a floured work surface and knead until smooth and elastic, about 10 minutes, adding only enough flour to prevent the dough from sticking. Shape the dough into a ball and transfer to a buttered bowl. Turn the dough to coat with butter. Cover bowl with plastic wrap and place in a warm, draft-free spot to rise until doubled in size, about 1 to 1½ hours.

Punch down the dough and divide into two equal pieces, if making loaves (or eight equal pieces if making rolls). Shape dough into balls. Place balls on buttered sheet pans, cover loosely, and let rise until doubled in size, about 1 hour. Preheat oven to 350ºF (290ºC). Beat the remaining egg. Brush the tops of the loaves (or rolls) with the beaten egg. Place dough on a baking sheet, and bake until the bread is a dark, shiny gold and sounds hollow when tapped on the top and bottom, about 30 minutes. Cool completely on racks before slicing.

[Makes 2 round loaves (or 8 rolls)]

Portuguese Sweet Bread

Living in Bristol, Rhode Island, I am surrounded by the influence of Portuguese cooking. This bread section wouldn't be complete if I didn't include a Portuguese sweet bread recipe. Sweet bread's greatest asset is its many uses. Don't just reserve this delicious bread for sandwiches—use it in your favorite French toast recipe, and for rich, delicate bread pudding.

[Makes 1 loaf]

Pumpernickel Bread

In my research and development of the perfect pumpernickel bread for sandwiches, I realized that it can be quite involved and somewhat difficult to make true pumpernickel. I borrowed this recipe from James Beard's *Beard on Bread*, an exhaustive, beautifully written book featuring numerous recipes for old-world breads. Mr. Beard preferred this recipe over others for its simplicity.

1 package active dry yeast (approx. 9 g)

1 tablespoon (15 g) granulated sugar

1⅓ cups (310 ml) warm water (100°F to 115°F [38°C–46°C])

2 tablespoons (40 g) molasses

2 tablespoons (60 ml) vegetable oil

1 tablespoon (18 g) salt

1 cup (125 g) all-purpose flour

1 cup (125 g) whole-wheat flour

2 cups (250 g) rye flour

½ cup (70 g) cornmeal

Combine the yeast, sugar, and ¼ cup (120 ml) warm water in a large mixing bowl. Let rest for 5 minutes until foamy. Add the molasses, oil, and salt, mixing well. Add the remaining cup (235 ml) water. Mix the flours and cornmeal together and add, 1 cup (125 g) at a time, to the yeast mixture, beating it in until you have a fairly stiff but workable dough; it will be quite sticky, heavy, and difficult to stir.

Turn dough onto a floured board and knead, adding more flour as necessary, until the dough becomes smooth and elastic, about 10 minutes or longer. Shape dough into a ball, place in a buttered bowl, and turn to coat with butter. Cover with plastic wrap and place in a warm, draft-free spot to rise until doubled in size, about 2 to 2½ hours. (The dough is quite heavy, so it takes much longer to rise than lighter breads). Punch down the dough and shape it into a loaf that will fit a well-buttered, 8" × 4" × 2" (20 × 10 × 5 cm) tin. Cover and let rise to the top of the pan, another 2 to 3 hours. Preheat oven to 375°F (190°C). Bake for 35 to 45 minutes, or until the loaf sounds hollow when tapped on top and bottom. Cool thoroughly on a rack before slicing.

Rosemary Focaccia

Focaccia is an Italian staple, originally enjoyed by old-world bakers as a snack in between the laborious efforts of bread baking. Focaccia has since made a name for itself as a premier sandwich loaf. This rustic recipe, with fresh rosemary throughout, can be made into two large loaves or smaller individual rounds for sandwiches.

2 cups warm water (about 90°F [35°C])

1½ tablespoons (18 g) active dry yeast

6 cups (750 g) unbleached all-purpose flour

4 teaspoons (24 g) salt

¼ cup (60 ml) olive oil

3 tablespoons (12 g) fresh rosemary, coarsely chopped

2 teaspoons (12 g) coarse sea salt or kosher salt

Whisk ½ cup (120 ml) of the water and the yeast together in the bowl of a heavy-duty mixer. Set the mixture aside for 5 minutes, until the yeast is dissolved and the mixture becomes creamy. Meanwhile, whisk the flour and salt together in a large bowl and set aside. Add 1½ cups (355 ml) water and the olive oil to the yeast mixture, whisk to blend. Add about half of the flour and 2 tablespoons (8 g) of the chopped fresh rosemary, and stir with a rubber spatula, until just mixed. Attach the dough hook to the mixer. Add the remaining flour and mix on low speed for about 3 minutes, until the dough just starts to come together. Add more warm water if the dough appears to be too dry or stiff. Increase the mixer speed to medium-high and continue to mix for about 10 minutes, scraping the sides and hook as needed, until the dough is soft, slightly moist, elastic, and rolls off the sides of the bowl. (Stretch a small piece of dough—if it remains intact and becomes almost transparent, it is done.)

Transfer the dough to a lightly floured work surface and shape it into a ball. Place dough in a well-oiled mixing bowl, and turn the dough to coat it completely with oil. Cover with plastic wrap and set aside in a warm, draft-free area to rise until doubled in size, about 45 minutes to 1 hour.

Punch the dough down, and let it rise until doubled in size again, about 45 minutes to 1 hour longer. Punch the dough down again, and turn it out onto a work surface. Cut the dough into two equal pieces for large loaves (or six smaller pieces to make rolls, or any combination of the two to make desired shapes). Shape each piece into a ball. Place each dough round into an individual, large, well-oiled, plastic zippered bag. Refrigerate for at least 24 hours.

About 1½ hours before you plan to bake the bread, remove the dough from the refrigerator. Discard plastic bags, place dough on a lightly floured work surface, dust the tops of the balls with flour, and cover loosely with plastic wrap. Let rest for about 1 hour, until the dough reaches a cool room temperature. Position the oven rack on the lower third of the oven with a baking stone. Preheat to 450°F (230°C).

Dust a peel with cornmeal, or, if not using a baking stone, line two baking sheets with parchment paper and dust the paper with cornmeal; set the baking sheets aside. Fill a spray bottle with water and set aside as well. Stretch the dough into two 10" (25 cm) rounds or six 6" (15 cm) rounds and let rest for about 10 minutes. Transfer dough to peel or the baking sheets. Brush the dough with olive oil and sprinkle with sea salt. Gently push bits of fresh rosemary into the bread with your fingers. Place in oven and bake for 15 to 20 minutes, until golden, spraying the oven with water three times during the first 8 minutes of baking. Remove peel or baking sheets from oven and brush immediately with olive oil. Allow focaccia to cool on a rack.

Focaccia is best eaten the day it is baked, but it may be wrapped airtight and frozen for up to two weeks. To serve after freezing, thaw while still wrapped, then heat in a 350°F (175°C) oven before serving.

Whole-Wheat Bread

Whole-wheat bread is a simple variation of white bread. With the addition of whole-wheat flour and olive oil for richness, these loaves are perfect for toasting and great sandwich making.

2¼ cups (530 ml) warm water (105°F to 115°F [45°C])

1 tablespoon (12 g) active dry yeast

1 tablespoon (15 g) granulated sugar

5 cups (625 g) whole-wheat flour

2 cups (250 g) bread flour or all-purpose flour

¼ cup (60 ml) olive oil

1 tablespoon (18 g) salt

4 tablespoons (55 g) unsalted butter, softened

Combine the yeast and sugar with ½ cup (120 ml) warm water in the bowl of a heavy-duty mixer, whisking to blend. Allow the mixture to rest until the yeast is foamy, about 5 minutes. Meanwhile, combine flours in a mixing bowl, whisking to incorporate. Attach dough hook to mixer. Add the remaining 1¾ cups (410 ml) water, olive oil, and about 3½ cups (435 g) flour to the yeast mixture. Turn the mixer on and off a few times to incorporate without tossing the flour out of the bowl. Mix on low speed, adding 3½ cups (435 g) more flour. Increase the mixer speed to medium and beat, stopping to scrape down the bowl and hook as needed, until the dough comes together. If necessary, add a bit more flour, 1 tablespoon (8 g) at a time, until the dough comes together. Add the salt and continue to beat and knead at medium speed for about 10 minutes, until the dough is smooth and elastic. When the dough is thoroughly mixed, add the butter, 1 tablespoon (14 g) at a time, and beat until it is incorporated. If the dough separates with the addition of the butter, don't be alarmed; this is expected—it will come back together with additional beating. Turn the dough out onto a lightly floured work surface and shape it into a ball. Place it in a large, well-oiled bowl, and turn the dough to coat completely with oil; cover with plastic wrap and place in a warm, draft-free spot to rise until doubled in size, about 45 minutes to an hour.

Butter two 8½" x 4½" x 2¾" (21 x 11 x 7 cm) loaf pans and set them aside. Turn dough onto a lightly floured work surface—this should deflate the dough—and divide in half. Working with one piece at a time, use your hands (or a rolling pin) to shape the dough into a large rectangle that measures 9" x 12" (23 x 30.5 cm). Starting at the top, with a short side facing you, fold the dough about two-thirds of the way down the rectangle, then fold it again, so that the top edge meets the bottom edge. Pinch the seam to seal it. Turn the roll so that the seam is in the center, facing up, and turn the ends in just enough so that the roll will fit in a buttered loaf pan. Pinch the seams to seal, then turn the loaf over, so the seam is on the bottom again, and, using the palms of your hands, plump the loaf to get an even shape. Drop the loaf into the pan, seam side down. Repeat the process with the remaining dough. Cover the loaves with oiled plastic wrap and place in a warm, draft-free spot to rise again, until doubled in size, about 45 minutes.

Meanwhile, center a rack in the oven, and preheat to 375°F (190°C). Bring 3 cups (705 ml) of water to a boil. Place water in a shallow, oven-proof baking pan, on the bottom rack of the oven. The steam released during baking will create a crisp crust. When the loaves have risen fully (test by poking a finger gently into the dough; the impression should remain), remove plastic wrap, and transfer loaf pans to the oven. Bake for 35 to 45 minutes, or until they are honey-brown in color, and an instant-read thermometer registers 200°F (95°C) when inserted deep into the center of a loaf. (Turn the dough out, and insert the thermometer from the bottom.)

If you'd like your loaves to be evenly brown, turn them out of the pans and bake them directly on the rack of the oven for the last 10 minutes of baking time. Otherwise, remove the loaves from their pans as soon as they come from the oven, and cool the breads on a rack. The loaves should not be cut until they are almost completely cool. Once completely cool, they can be stored in a brown paper bag for up to two days, or be frozen in airtight bags for up to one month. Thaw at room temperature before using.

[Meat]

If you've visited your local deli counter recently, you're probably well aware of the wide variety of cold cuts available, not to mention other choices such as barbecued pork, grilled chicken, or cooked seafood. Meat, like bread, is a personal choice that really relies on the other ingredients around it to make the whole sandwich. When building a sandwich, keep in mind the flavor and the texture of the meat you select, as well the cooking temperature (if any) and preparation methods.

If you are making sandwiches ahead of time, food safety is paramount. Make sure all sandwiches made with meat and cold cuts are kept as cold as possible; meat can spoil under adverse temperatures, so I recommend using ice or cold packs to keep the sandwiches fresh and safe.

When traveling, I recommend packing all your sandwich ingredients separately and building the sandwich once you reach your destination, but in some cases, this won't be practical. If you pack everything separately, be sure to bring along condiments and utensils, and keep all ingredients well chilled in airtight containers.

[Vegetables]

The main question relating to vegetables is whether they are used raw or cooked. Both types work fine for sandwich making, but, as with all ingredients, make sure they complement each other. The cut of the vegetable is also important. Slicing certain vegetables too thick will make the sandwich hard to eat, while if you slice them too thin, the flavors will be lost. If using grilled vegetables, I recommend a ¼-inch (6 mm) thick slice, so the vegetables, don't cook too fast and/or fall apart. Certain vegetables such as lettuce, should always be used raw, but spinach works fine served raw or cooked.

The following ingredients appear in several recipes and are excellent options for many of your own recipes.

Roasted Peppers

One pepper makes about ½ cup (120 g) of sliced roasted pepper

Any bell pepper variety— red, yellow, orange, green, or purple—works well for roasting.

The easiest way to roast peppers is by using a gas grill. Preheat the grill to high. Coat the peppers evenly with olive oil and place on the grill. Cook the peppers until the skin is charred black, turning them periodically to ensure even roasting. If you do not have a gas grill, I recommend using the broiler in your oven. Preheat the broiler, then place the oiled

peppers in a shallow roasting pan under the broiler on the middle rack of the oven. Broil until skin is black, turning them occasionally to ensure even roasting.

Once the skin is charred black, transfer the peppers to a paper or plastic bag. Seal the bag and set aside for 5 minutes. Remove peppers from the bag and remove blackened skin, slice, and remove seeds. Use roasted peppers immediately, or refrigerate for up to 5 days.

Roasted Garlic

Roasting garlic is a technique that concentrates the flavors of raw garlic into an intense, robust, earthy flavor and aroma. Like truffle oil, the flavor and smell of roasted garlic is distinctive and easily recognizable. If you don't like the taste of raw garlic, I encourage you to try this technique, as roasted garlic is unique and enjoyable.

Makes about ½ cup (120 g)

4 heads fresh garlic, stem ends removed to ½" (1.25 cm)

2 tablespoons (30 ml) olive oil

Salt

Coarse ground black pepper

Preheat the oven to 375°F (190°C). Place the garlic, cut ends up, in an oven-safe pan or dish. Drizzle each head with olive oil and season with salt and pepper. Place in oven and roast for 30 to 45 minutes or until garlic is a rich brown, caramelized color and the cloves are easily pierced with the sharp tip of a knife. Remove from oven and let cool. If not using immediately, store refrigerated in an airtight container for up to one week. If using immediately, remove the roasted cloves by pinching the ends of each clove to force the garlic from the skin.

[Cheese]
Cheese is my favorite part of a sandwich. It's a bit more complicated than some other ingredients, however, because of the differences from one variety to another. When selecting cheese, keep in mind its texture, melting ability, spreadability, and flavor intensity. Melting ability is obviously critical if you are making a hot sandwich. Some varieties of cheese just don't melt well and others can be too runny. Swiss cheese, for example, is used in a Reuben because the flavor is strong enough to pair well with the robust flavors of rye bread, sauerkraut, and corned beef, while its melting ability makes it soft but not runny. Spreading cheeses—such as cream cheese, Boursin, and goat cheese— also make great additions to a sandwich. These three types of cheese offer intense flavors with a subtle texture that lend themselves well to certain applications, but goat cheese and Boursin do not melt well. My advice? Know who you are serving, as many cheeses require an acquired taste.

[Spreads and Condiments]
Think of spreads and condiments as the glue that holds the sandwich together. There are literally hundreds of packaged condiments and spreads available for use on sandwiches, but I believe homemade is still the best. Don't be afraid to experiment. As with any sandwich ingredient, the main thing to keep in mind is that all the elements work well together.

[Sandwich Construction]
The layers of a sandwich speak volumes about the maker and the eater. It's said there's even a secret society that believes in the art of interpreting a sandwich, its contents, and how they relate to the eater or the builder. While I can't teach you the psychology of the sandwich, I will stress that the order in which you assemble a sandwich can be crucial to the enjoyment. If your tomatoes slip out, it's a big mess. Cheese placed in the middle of a sandwich won't melt, and lettuce belongs around everything else. While there is no real science behind the construction of a sandwich, after making hundreds for this book, here's my definition of the right order:

1. Bread
2. Condiment
3. Cheese—if hot
4. Lettuce—if cold
5. Cheese—if cold
6. Tomato or other vegetable
7. Meat
8. Cheese again—if cold
9. Lettuce again—if cold
10. Cheese again—if hot
11. Condiment
12. Bread

[Making the Sandwiches]
Each of the recipes in this book instructs you on how to make one sandwich using the ingredients called for in the recipe. After completing one sandwich, the recipe will instruct you to repeat the process to assemble the remaining sandwiches. Take care to split the ingredients evenly among all the sandwiches.

chapter 2

Hot and Grilled Sandwiches

The word *panini* is actually the Italian term for sandwich. Because of the popularity of the Italian technique of grilling or pressing a sandwich to heat and toast it, panini has been adapted to refer specifically to this style of hot sandwich. Throughout this book, I refer to panini as sandwiches that are pressed or grilled. Whether you use a panini grill or a stovetop skillet, the technique is simple. Build your sandwich with the appropriate ingredients, spread oil or butter on the outside of both sides of the bread, and grill or toast.

1 lb (455 g) honey-baked deli ham, sliced thin

8 slices Swiss cheese

6 ounces (170 g) baby spinach

Whole Grain Molasses Mustard (see page112)

Shaved-Apple Salad (recipe follows)

Butter, room temperature

8 slices pumpernickel bread

FOR SHAVED-APPLE SALAD:

Makes about 2 cups (475 ml)

½ cup (112 g) mayonnaise

1 tablespoon (14 g) sour cream

1 tablespoon (20 g) honey

1 tablespoon (15 ml) cider vinegar

1 teaspoon (3 g) brown sugar

1 cup (90 g) red cabbage, thinly sliced

½ red onion, thinly sliced

1 Granny Smith apple, peeled, cored, and grated on the coarse grate of a box grater, then tossed with the juice of 1 lemon

1 tablespoon (6 g) fresh chopped mint

Salt

Coarse ground black pepper

Preheat the panini grill or stovetop skillet to medium. Lay pumpernickel bread on a clean, flat, and dry work surface. Spread one slice of bread with molasses mustard, then layer with ham, spinach, apple salad, and two slices Swiss cheese. Spread molasses mustard on second bread slice and top sandwich. Butter both sides of sandwich and grill for about 7 minutes on each side or until browned and crisp and cheese is melted. (Sandwich may also be individually wrapped in aluminum foil and baked at 400°F [200°C] for about 20 minutes.) Repeat process with remaining ingredients to make additional sandwiches. Remove from heat, slice, and serve warm.

[For shaved-apple salad]
Combine mayonnaise, sour cream, honey, cider vinegar, and brown sugar in medium bowl and stir. Add cabbage, onion, apple, and mint and toss until well incorporated, then season with salt and pepper. Set aside until ready for assembly.

[Makes 4 sandwiches]

Honey-Baked Ham Panini with Shaved-Apple Salad

The combination of apples and baked or roasted ham is phenomenal at any time of year, but it is especially welcome in autumn. A traditional coleslaw recipe is given a crisp, tangy twist with the addition of apples, which complement the honey-baked ham perfectly.

Southwestern Spicy Beef Panini with Black Bean Pesto

The flavors that the Southwest provides are brilliant. This is a classic steak and cheese gone south of the border.

2 tablespoons (30 ml) olive oil

1 pound (455 g) shaved beef sirloin

1 small red onion, thinly sliced

1 tablespoon (10 g) chopped fresh garlic

Parsley, chopped (to taste)

1½ tablespoons (20 ml) chili-garlic sauce*

8 slices of ciabatta bread or favorite hearty sandwich bread

1 roasted red pepper, thinly sliced (see recipe, page 28)

6 ounces (170 g) Monterey Jack cheese, shredded

*Chili-garlic sauce can be found in Asian markets or the Asian section of your local grocery store.

BLACK BEAN PESTO:

2 tablespoons (20 g) minced garlic

2 Serrano chilies, seeded and minced

1 (14-ounce [400 g]) can black beans, rinsed and drained

1 tablespoon (15 ml) rice vinegar

2 tablespoons (30 ml) olive oil

2 tablespoons (4 g) chopped fresh cilantro

1 green onion, chopped

1 tablespoon (7 g) ground cumin

3 drops chipotle pepper sauce (Tabasco brand is good quality)

Heat olive oil in a medium sauté pan over medium-high heat. Sauté beef, red onion, and garlic for about 3 minutes. Add chili-garlic sauce and continue cooking for an additional 4 minutes, until beef is cooked through. Add chopped parsley and season with salt and pepper. Remove from heat, set aide.

Preheat stovetop grill pan or electric panini grill. Working on a flat, clean, and dry surface, lay out 4 slices of bread. Spread each slice with black bean pesto, top with beef mixture, roasted red pepper, and shredded Monterey Jack cheese; finish with remaining slice of bread. Spread butter evenly over top slices. Place sandwich on grilling surface, butter side down, butter additional sides and cook. If working on a panini-style electric grill, cook for 10 minutes. If working on a stovetop grill pan, cook for about 5 minutes on each side, until browned and crisp. Remove from heat, let rest for 3 minutes, then slice in half and serve.

[For the black bean pesto] Working in the bowl of a food processor fitted with the blade attachment, add all the ingredients. Process until ingredients are chopped and well combined. Remove and set aside.

Sandwiches, Panini, and Wraps

2 cups (100 g) packed fresh basil leaves, blanched, plus 24 additional leaves (not blanched)

1 cup (235 ml) extra-virgin olive oil

Salt and coarse ground black pepper

1 loaf ciabatta bread or panini bread, sliced about ½-inch (1 cm) thick

2 cloves roasted garlic (see recipe, page 29)

1 pound (455 g) buffalo mozzarella cheese, cut into 18 slices

Butter at room temperature

[Makes 6 sandwiches]

Italian Grilled Cheese
Panini **with Basil Oil**

Italians love their tomatoes and mozzarella. What better a way to enjoy them than between two crisp, toasted pieces of bread with basil oil? Any good-quality melting cheese can be used in this panini, but the rich, velvety texture of fresh mozzarella truly celebrates the Italian flavor. Use garden-fresh basil for the basil oil to add zip to the flavors.

In the bowl of a food processor fitted with the blade attachment, place the blanched basil and olive oil. Blend on high until all the basil is chopped and oil appears bright green. Strain oil through a fine sieve or cheesecloth into a bowl, season with salt and black pepper, and set aside.

Preheat stovetop grill pan or electric panini grill. Working on a flat, clean, and dry work surface, lay out 6 slices of bread. Spread roasted garlic on each slice of bread. Divide mozzarella cheese slices among the 6 slices of bread, layering evenly. Top with sliced tomato and reserved basil leaves. Drizzle tomatoes with basil oil. Top with remaining 6 slices of bread.

Spread butter on top pieces, coating bread evenly. Place sandwiches on grilling surface, butter side down, then butter additional side and cook. If working on a panini-style electric grill, lower lid and cook for 10 minutes. If working on a stovetop grill pan, cook for about 5 minutes on each side, until browned and crisp. Remove from heat, let rest for 3 minutes, then slice in half and serve.

5 tablespoons (75 ml) vegetable oil, divided

⅓ cup (40 g) minced celery

4 green onions, minced

½ cup (58 g) dried bread crumbs

1 lb (455 g) lump crab meat, picked over for any shell

1 egg

2 tablespoons (8 g) minced parsley

¼ cup (15 g) fresh chopped cilantro

1 red bell pepper, diced

⅓ cup (75 g) mayonnaise

1 cup (240 ml) Grilled Onion Relish (see recipe, page 110)

½ cup (120 ml) Spicy Tartar Sauce (see recipe, page 110)

4 onion sandwich rolls, grilled in a panini grill

Heat 3 tablespoons (45 ml) vegetable oil in a sauté pan. Add celery, green onion, and red pepper, then sauté until tender, about 3 minutes. Add bread crumbs and brown for one minute. Remove from heat and transfer to mixing bowl, and let cool for 10 minutes. Add crab, egg, parsley, cilantro, and mayonnaise, stir to combine, then season with salt and pepper. Form crab mixture into 4-inch (10 cm) balls, then flatten into a disk shape. (The crab cakes should fit comfortably on the onion roll.)

Preheat oven to 400°F (200°C). Heat 2 tablespoons (30 ml) vegetable oil in a large sauté pan over medium heat. Add crab cakes and cook until well done, about 7 minutes per side. Repeat the process, adding oil as necessary, to cook all the crab cakes. Transfer cakes to a sheet pan and bake in oven for 10 minutes. Remove from oven and place crab cake on bottom half of onion roll, then top with generous amount of tartar sauce, onion relish, and top half of roll. Repeat process with remaining ingredients to make additional sandwiches. Serve.

[Makes 4 sandwiches]

Crab Cake Panini with Grilled Onion Relish and Spicy Tartar Sauce

Crab cakes, while good on their own, can take on a new life as a panini. This one is no exception; the burst of flavor from the onion relish is very satisfying. If you prefer a more health-conscious version, serve the crab cake on a bed of greens without the bread.

1 italian eggplant, sliced horizontally into 1/2" (1.3 cm)-thick slices

1 small zucchini, sliced horizontally into 1/2" (1.3 cm)-thick slices

1 red pepper, roasted and sliced (see recipe, page 28)

1 red onion, sliced into 1/2" (1.3 cm)-thick slices

2 portobello mushroom caps, stems trimmed

1/2 cup (120 ml) olive oil, plus extra for brushing

Salt

Coarse ground black pepper

8 slices crusty ciabatta or other sandwich bread

4 pieces red leaf lettuce

1/3 cup (75 ml) Herbed Feta Spread (see recipe, page 113)

Balsamic vinegar

Preheat outdoor grill or stove-top grill pan to medium-high. Brush eggplant, zucchini, onion slices, and portobello mushrooms evenly with olive oil, then season with salt and pepper. Place on hot grill and cook until browned and tender, about 4 minutes per side for eggplant and zucchini, 6 minutes per side for the onion, and 8 minutes per side for the mushrooms. Remove from grill or pan and let cool. Peel the purple skin from the eggplant slices. Cut the onion rings in half.

Preheat the panini grill or skillet to medium. Lay out bread, spread bottom with herbed feta spread, and layer with eggplant, lettuce, zucchini, onion, mushroom, and red pepper. Spread second bread slice with feta spread and place on top of sandwich, feta side down. Brush both sides of sandwich evenly and generously with olive oil, and grill, about 10 minutes if using panini grill and 7 minutes per side if using skillet. If using skillet, cover sandwich with a small piece of aluminum foil and place a heavier skillet or stone on the foil to press the sandwich while it cooks.

Repeat process with remaining ingredients to make additional sandwiches. Slice and serve warm.

[Makes 4 sandwiches]

Grilled Vegetable Panini with Herbed Feta Spread

Grilling vegetables results in very concentrated, robust flavors that work well in a sandwich.

- 4 tablespoons (55 g) butter
- 2 tablespoons (30 ml) olive oil, plus additional for brushing
- 2 small, sweet yellow onions, sliced thin
- 1 lb (455 g) assorted wild mushrooms, sliced
- 1 teaspoon (5 g) sugar
- 1 tablespoon (3 g) lemon thyme
- Salt
- Coarse ground black pepper
- 6 ounces (170 g) fontina cheese, sliced
- 4 ounces (115 g) fresh buffalo mozzarella cheese, sliced
- 12 slices crusty ciabatta bread

Melt butter and olive oil in a large skillet over medium-high heat. Sauté onions, stirring occasionally. When the onions begin to wilt, reduce the heat to medium and add the mushrooms and sugar. Toss to combine, then continue to sauté, stirring occasionally until mixture becomes a dark caramel color, about 10 minutes. (Reduce heat if the onions and mushrooms become crisp; they should remain tender.) Add lemon thyme and toss to combine, then remove from heat and set aside.

Preheat panini grill or skillet to medium. Place bread on a flat, clean, and dry work surface, then layer with fontina and mozzarella cheeses. Add second slice of bread, brush top with olive oil, and place, oiled side down, on grilling surface. Grill until cheese is melted and bread is browned and crisp, about 10 minutes if using panini grill or 7 minutes per side if using skillet. If using skillet, place a heavier skillet or stone on the sandwich to press it while it cooks. Repeat process with remaining ingredients to make additional sandwiches.

Keep the first batch warm in a 200°F (90°C) oven. Pull sandwiches apart and insert onion/mushroom mixture, then close, slice, and serve warm.

[Makes 6 sandwiches]

Fontina Panini with Caramelized Onion and Mushroom Relish

Fontina is a great melting cheese with an intense, almost earthy flavor that lends itself nicely to the flavors of assorted wild mushrooms. The choice of mushrooms is up to you, but I recommend shitake, oyster, and porcini.

6 large fresh butter croissants, sliced open horizontally

1 1/2 lb (680 g) honey-baked or smoked deli ham, thinly sliced

6 slices Swiss cheese, thinly sliced

1/3 cup (80 g) Dijon mustard

3 tablespoons (45 ml) butter, softened

1 teaspoon (2 g) fresh chopped chives

1/4 teaspoon (.5 g) coarse ground black pepper

Baked Ham and Swiss on Croissant with Dijon Butter

This is a deliciously quick and simple dish that combines the subtle flavor of butter with Dijon mustard, ham, and Swiss cheese.

Preheat oven to 375°F (190°C). Combine mustard with butter in a small bowl, then mix thoroughly using a fork. Add chives and pepper, stir to combine, then set aside but do not refrigerate. Lay bottom half of croissant out on a flat, clean, and dry work surface, then spread with Dijon butter. Layer with one slice Swiss cheese, ham, and second slice of Swiss cheese. Spread the inside of the croissant top with Dijon butter. Close the sandwich, wrap it in aluminum foil, place on a sheet pan, and bake until cheese is melted and croissant begins to turn crisp, about 20 minutes. Repeat process with remaining ingredients to make additional sandwiches. Remove, unwrap, and serve hot.

Grilled Tuna Panini **with Wasabi Ginger Mayonnaise**

This delicious summer sandwich pairs grilled tuna steaks with wasabi mayonnaise. Tuna steaks on the grill are a special indulgence. The sauce or marinade for tuna steaks needs only to be subtle to enhance the flavor. Tuna paired with wasabi mayonnaise ensures a perfect summer sandwich.

4 ($\frac{1}{4}$-lb [115 g]) tuna steaks	4 portuguese english muffins
$\frac{1}{4}$ cup (60 ml) extra-virgin olive oil	$\frac{1}{4}$ cup (112 g) prepared mayonnaise
1 teaspoon (2 g) coarse ground black pepper	1 tablespoon (15 g) wasabi paste
$\frac{1}{2}$ teaspoon (3 g) kosher salt	1 teaspoon (3 g) freshly grated ginger
$\frac{1}{2}$ teaspoon (.5 g) dried lemongrass (optional)	$\frac{1}{2}$ teaspoon (2.5 ml) lemon juice
	4 leaves Bibb lettuce
	1 english cucumber, thinly sliced

Preheat outdoor grill or stovetop grill pan to high. Combine olive oil, pepper, salt, and lemongrass in a small mixing bowl. Brush each tuna steak on both sides with the olive oil mixture. Place on hot grill and cook until browned but still pink in the middle, about 7 minutes per side. Combine mayonnaise, wasabi paste, ginger, and lemon juice in a second mixing bowl, stir to combine, and refrigerate for at least 30 minutes. Preheat panini grill or skillet. Butter both sides of roll and grill until toasted on both sides, about 5 minutes. Lay out bottom roll and layer with lettuce, cucumber, wasabi mayonnaise, and tuna steak. Add remaining mayonnaise and top of roll. Repeat process with remaining ingredients to make additional sandwiches. Serve.

4 (8-ounce [225 g])
boneless, skinless chicken breasts

olive oil

1 tablespoon (6 g) coarse
ground black pepper

2 tablespoons (20 g)
chopped fresh garlic

2 medium red peppers

1/2 lb (225 g) sharp
provolone cheese, thinly sliced

8 ounces (225 g)
mozzarella cheese, thinly sliced

12 leaves fresh basil

8 ounces (225 g) sliced pepperoni

6 ciabatta rolls

1/4 cup (60 ml) Roasted
Garlic Aioli (see recipe, page 111)

Preheat grill to high. Combine chicken breasts with 4 tablespoons (60 ml) olive oil, pepper, and garlic. On a platter, rub each red pepper generously with olive oil. Place chicken and red peppers on grill. Grill chicken 7 minutes on each side, until browned and cooked through (the internal temperature should reach 165°F [75°C]). Transfer chicken to a cutting board and let cool. When cool enough to handle, cut into thin strips and set aside.

Grill red peppers, charring the skin black all over, about 20 minutes total. Transfer to a paper bag and seal, then let sit for about 5 minutes. Remove peppers from bag and peel away charred skin, leaving bright red flesh. Remove stem, seeds, and pulp, then cut into thick strips and set aside.

Brush inside of roll with olive oil, place on grill, oiled side down, and toast until golden brown. Transfer to plate. Lay out bottom half of roll, toasted side up, and spread with garlic aioli. Top with provolone, basil, pepperoni, chicken, red pepper, mozzarella, and finally top of roll, toasted side down. Wrap sandwich in aluminum foil. Reduce heat on grill to low. Place sandwich on grill and cook for 7 minutes, turning once, until cheese is melted. Repeat process with remaining ingredients to make additional sandwiches. Remove from foil, slice in half, and serve.

[Makes 6 sandwiches]

Chicken Soprano Panini

I'm sure Tony Soprano would enjoy this sandwich, which is so named for the Italian meats and cheeses found within.

[Makes 4 sandwiches]

Pickled Pastrami Panini

The traditional pastrami on rye sandwich is one of my favorites, and there is no substitution for good-quality pastrami. Here, pickles, mustard, and pastrami are united on this grilled panini, in a mouth-watering tribute to a classic.

8 slices farmhouse loaf or multigrain bread

¹/₃ cup (75 ml) Dijon mustard

1 lb (455 g) pastrami, hickory smoked or peppered, thinly sliced

2 kosher-style pickles, cut lengthwise into thin slices

¹/₄ lb (115 g) Swiss cheese

olive oil for brushing

Preheat panini grill or skillet to medium. Place bread on a clean, flat, and dry work surface and spread with Dijon mustard. Top with 1 slice Swiss cheese, pastrami, pickles, remaining slice of Swiss cheese, and top half of bread. Brush top with olive oil, then place sandwich on panini grill or in skillet, oiled side down, and brush top with olive oil. Grill until bread is browned and crisp and cheese is melted, about 10 minutes if using panini grill or 7 minutes per side if using skillet. If using skillet, place a heavier skillet or stone on the sandwich to press it while it cooks. Repeat process with remaining ingredients to make additional sandwiches. Remove from grill, slice, and serve.

[Makes 4 sandwiches]

Paris Texas Panini

I think Texas is the only place you can visit Paris, London, and Rome and never leave the United States. This panini, however, brings together an assortment of international flavors. When buying hot sauce, I recommend a brand called Chilulah.

1 french baguette

3 (6-ounce [170 g]) boneless, skinless chicken breasts

1 (6-ounce [170 g]) can green enchilada sauce

1 teaspoon (5 ml) hot sauce

1 teaspoon (2 g) cumin

¼ teaspoon (.3 g) dried oregano

1 teaspoon (2 g) coarse ground black pepper

3 tablespoons (30 g) chopped fresh garlic

8 ounces (225 g) Monterey Jack cheese, sliced

6 ounces (170 g) monchego cheese, sliced

4 poblano peppers

1 large white onion, thinly sliced

Olive oil

Preheat grill to high. Combine enchilada sauce, hot sauce, cumin, oregano, pepper, and garlic in a large bowl, and stir to combine. Add chicken, toss to coat, then cover and refrigerate for at least 30 minutes. Rub poblano peppers and onions with olive oil and place on hot grill. Grill onions about 4 minutes on each side until browned. Remove and set aside. Grill peppers, charring all sides until skin is black and blistered, about 15 minutes. Transfer to a paper bag and seal, then let sit for about 5 minutes. Remove peppers from bag and peel away charred skin. Remove stem, seeds, and pulp, then set aside.

Remove chicken from refrigerator and grill for about 7 minutes on each side, until cooked through and browned (the internal temperature should reach 165°F [75°C]). Remove from grill and set aside.

Preheat panini grill or skillet. Cut baguette into four equal pieces, then slice each piece horizontally, taking care not to cut all the way through. Fold bread open and with inside facing up, press down to flatten. Turn bread to work with what would be the outside of the loaf. On bottom half of bread, layer monchego and Monterey Jack cheeses. Close bread inside out. Spread butter on top half and grill until browned and cheese is melted through, about 5 minutes. Meanwhile, slice chicken in thin strips with the grain and set aside. Remove sandwiches from grill. Open up and layer with poblano peppers, onion, and chicken. Close sandwich and slice in half. Repeat process with remaining ingredients to make additional sandwiches. Serve warm.

[Makes 6 sandwiches]

Bacon Cheddar Panini on Raisin Bread

I really enjoy the savory flavor of pepper-smoked bacon combined with the sweetness of raisins. This sandwich makes a great hurry-up-and-go breakfast, combining the sweet and savory with melted cheddar cheese. The kids will love this one on the way to school.

12 slices thick, peppered or smoked bacon, cooked

6 ounces (170 g) sharp white cheddar cheese, sliced

12 slices raisin bread

3 tablespoons (45 g) butter, room temperature

Preheat panini grill or stovetop skillet. Place raisin bread on flat, clean, and dry work surface. Layer with cheddar cheese, bacon, more cheddar cheese, and second bread slice. Butter both sides of sandwich and grill until browned and crisp and cheese is melted, about 10 minutes. Repeat process with remaining ingredients to make additional sandwiches. Serve.

12 slices rye bread

4 tablespoons (60 g)
butter, softened

1 cup (225 g) prepared
russian dressing

2 tablespoons (30 g)
german-style mustard

1½ lbs (680 g) deli pastrami
or corned beef, thinly sliced

½ lb (225 g)
Gruyere cheese, sliced

1 cup (225 g) sauerkraut

[Makes 6 sandwiches]

Irish Reuben Panini

It may be a culture clash to call a
Reuben a panini, but this multicultural
sandwich sure is good.

Preheat large ovenproof skillet over medium-high heat. Preheat oven to 375°F (190°C). Working on a clean, flat, and dry surface, lay out rye bread. Spread with russian dressing, then layer Gruyere cheese, pastrami, sauerkraut, and more pastrami, Gruyere cheese, and russian dressing. Top with a second slice of bread. Butter both sides of bread and cook until one side is browned, about 5 minutes. Flip sandwich over and place in oven to melt cheese. Repeat process with remaining ingredients to make additional sandwiches. Remove from oven, slice, and serve.

Pressed Cubano Chicken Sandwich

A staple of the Cuban population of Tampa and Miami, Florida, the Cubano is traditionally served on Cuban bread with roast pork and ham. My version combines roasted chicken with bacon on a sweet Hawaiian or Portuguese roll. If you are lucky enough to live in an area in which Cuban bread is available, then you may stick to the classic, but don't be afraid to experiment with a new twist.

1 teaspoon (5 ml) olive oil

1 garlic clove, minced

4 portuguese sweet rolls or hawaiian rolls, sliced in half horizontally

3 tablespoons (45 g) yellow mustard

2 tablespoons (32 g) sweet pickle relish

8 slices (½ ounce [15 g] each) Swiss cheese

8 slices bacon, cooked

¼ cup (5 g) whole cilantro leaves

6 ounces (170 g) oven-roasted ham, thinly sliced

6 ounces (170 g) roasted chicken breast, thinly sliced

Preheat stovetop grill or panini grill pan to medium heat. Combine oil and garlic in small bowl and set aside. Combine mustard and sweet relish in second bowl. Spread bottom half of each roll evenly with mustard/relish mixture. Layer with Swiss cheese, bacon, cilantro leaves, ham, chicken, and top half of roll. Grill until bread is toasted and cheese is melted, about 10 minutes if using panini grill, or 7 minutes per side if using stovetop skillet. Remove from grill and let sit for 5 minutes. Repeat process with remaining ingredients to make additional sandwiches. Cut each in half and served stacked with skewered banana peppers.

3 (6-ounce [170 g])
boneless, skinless
chicken breasts

6 stems lemon thyme

1 lemon, sliced in half lengthwise
and then cut into thin slices

6 Roma tomatoes

olive oil

coarse ground black pepper

Kosher salt

1 large parisian loaf,
ends removed, cut in quarters

4 tablespoons (60 g)
butter, room temperature

6 ounces (170 g) creamy
Havarti cheese, sliced

½ cup (120 ml) ricotta cheese

2 ounces (60 g) frisée or
other leafy greens

4 stems fresh italian flat-leaf
parsley

[Makes 4 sandwiches]

Lemon Thyme–Roasted Chicken Panini with Havarti and Oven-Dried Tomatoes

Lemon thyme is an herb that is not always readily available in the grocery stores, but it adds tremendous flavor to many dishes. I recommend buying lemon thyme seeds or seedlings in late spring, when the garden shops stock up with herbs for the garden. Even potted, it will grow quickly and heartily and will then be available all summer long for cooking.

Preheat oven to 400°F (200°C). Coat an ovenproof skillet (preferably cast iron) with non-stick cooking spray. Clean and butterfly chicken breasts horizontally. Fold each chicken breast open, top with two stems of lemon thyme and 3 slices of lemon, sprinkle with kosher salt and pepper, and close. Repeat with remaining chicken breasts. Place chicken breasts in skillet and drizzle with olive oil. Roast in oven until cooked through and browned on top, about 45 minutes. Remove and let cool, then remove thyme stems and lemon slices. Slice chicken into thin strips, cutting with the grain, and set aside.

Remove stem end of tomatoes. Line a sheet pan with parchment paper and coat with nonstick cooking spray. Cut tomatoes into ¼-inch (0.6 cm)-thick slices from top to bottom. Place on parchment paper and sprinkle with salt and pepper. Roast in 400°F (200°C) oven until shriveled and partially dried, about 45 minutes. Remove and set aside to cool.

Preheat panini grill or stovetop skillet. Slice loaves in half horizontally, taking care not to cut all the way through. Gently fold loaves open with both hands. Lay on flat surface with the inside of the bread facing up, then press firmly down on the loaf to flatten it. Layer bottom half with havarti and ricotta cheeses. Close bread, butter one side, and place on grill, buttered side down. Butter remaining side, then grill until browned and cheese is melted, about 5 minutes if using panini grill. If using stovetop skillet, do not butter remaining side. While grilling, place a heavier skillet or stone on the sandwich to weigh it down while it cooks. Grill for 5 minutes, then butter top, flip, and repeat. Transfer sandwiches to a plate, open and insert oven-dried tomatoes, sliced chicken, and greens. Repeat process with remaining ingredients to make additional sandwiches. Close sandwich, cut in half, and serve.

3 tablespoons (45 g) unsalted butter

1/4 cup (60 ml) extra-virgin olive oil, plus 3 tablespoons (45 ml)

2 (10-ounce [284 g]) packages bella or crimini mushrooms, cleaned and cut in quarters

1 cup (100 g) sliced shitake mushrooms

8 cloves garlic, minced and then divided

1 teaspoon (1 g) fresh chopped thyme

1 tablespoon (15 ml) balsamic vinegar

1/2 teaspoon (1 g) coarse ground black pepper

1/2 teaspoon (3 g) kosher salt

1 ciabatta loaf, sliced into 1/2" (1.3 cm)-thick slices

1/2 cup (75 g) mascarpone cheese

8 ounces (225 g) fontina cheese, thinly sliced

Preheat oven broiler. In a large skillet over medium-high heat, melt the butter and add 3 tablespoons (45 ml) olive oil. When hot, add 4 cloves minced garlic and bella and shitake mushrooms. Saute for 3 minutes, then add thyme, pepper, salt, and balsamic vinegar and cook for 3 additional minutes or until mushrooms are tender but not soft. Remove from heat and set aside.

Combine remaining minced garlic with remaining olive oil in a small bowl. Brush one side of 8 slices of bread with olive oil/garlic mixture, lay on sheet pan and toast under broiler on middle rack until browned, about 3 minutes. Remove, spread with mascarpone, and top with fontina. Place under broiler on middle rack until cheese is melted, about 3 minutes. Remove, top with mushroom mixture, and serve warm.

[Makes 6 sandwiches]

Open-Faced Fontina Melt

In my mind, the concept of an open-faced sandwich is really a contradiction in terms. Regardless, this recipe is so tasty that I had to share it. For hors d'oeuvres, prepare this sandwich on smaller slices of a baguette.

2 large parisian baguettes, ends removed, cut in half

1½ cups (355 ml) Béchamel Sauce (recipe follows)

12 ounces (340 g) white sharp cheddar cheese, thinly sliced

2 lb (1 kg) deli-sliced black forest ham

3 tablespoons (45 g) butter, melted

BÉCHAMEL SAUCE:

Makes about 2 cups

3 tablespoons (45 g) unsalted butter

3 tablespoons (24 g) flour

1 cup (235 ml) dry white wine

1 cup (235 ml) whole milk

1 tablespoon (15 g) Dijon mustard

¼ teaspoon (.5 g) nutmeg

salt

white pepper

Croque Monsieur Montréal

On a recent trip to Montreal, I was reintroduced to the Croque Monsieur, a truly gourmet ham and cheese sandwich topped with Béchamel sauce.

Preheat broiler. Slice baguettes in half horizontally. Open baguette and brush inside with melted butter. Place on a sheet pan and toast under broiler until browned, about 1 minute, then remove and set aside. On bottom half of bread, spread Béchamel sauce followed by cheddar cheese, then place under broiler to melt the cheese, about 2 minutes. Remove and top with ham and remaining cheddar cheese. Return to broiler once more to melt cheese, about 3 minutes. Remove, transfer to plate, top with top half of bread, and fold sandwich closed. Repeat process with remaining ingredients to make additional sandwiches. Serve warm with thin cut french fries.

[For béchamel sauce]
Scald the milk in a medium-sized saucepan over medium heat, stirring occasionally, until bubbles form around the sides, then turn off the heat. Melt the butter in a medium-sized skillet over medium-high heat. Add flour to butter, whisking thoroughly to combine. Cook until just turning tan in color, stirring constantly, about 3 minutes. Once roux has reached a light tan color, reduce heat to low, add the white wine, and stir vigorously to incorporate without leaving lumps. Once sauce is thick, gradually add scalded milk, ⅓ cup (75 ml) at a time, stirring vigorously and continuously between additions to prevent lumps. Add Dijon mustard and nutmeg and season with salt and pepper. The sauce is done when it coats the back of a wooden spoon. If it appears too thick, add more milk.

Inside-Out French Grilled Cheese

Turning a french baguette inside out gives you a better grilling surface for the bread.

6 (6-inch [15 cm])-long french baguettes

8 ounces (225 g) fresh buffalo mozzarella cheese, sliced thin

8 ounces (225 g) sliced provolone cheese

4 sprigs fresh tarragon, leaves removed and kept whole

2 tablespoons (28 g) butter, room temperature

Preheat panini grill or skillet to medium. Slice the baguette horizontally, taking care not to cut all the way through. Fold the baguette inside out. Top with mozzarella cheese and provolone, then sprinkle with fresh tarragon. Close baguette, butter both sides of the outside of the baguette, and place on a grill or in pan. Grill until the outsides are toasted and golden, about 3 minutes if using panini grill, or 1 to 2 minutes if using skillet. Remove from grill or pan and let sit for about 3 minutes. Repeat process with remaining ingredients to make additional baguettes. Serve warm.

Peppered Pastrami Panini with Apples and Brie

Brie cheese is really very underrated. It's a great melting cheese, and it really adds a unique flavor to food. Paired with apples and peppered salami, Brie takes on a new life.

12 slices dark rye or pumpernickel bread

1 lb (455 g) Brie cheese

6 ounces (170 g) creamy Havarti cheese, sliced

2 Granny Smith apples, peeled, cored, and thinly sliced

6 tablespoons (90 g) butter, softened

1 lb (455 g) peppered salami, thinly sliced

3 ounces (85 g) baby spinach

Preheat panini grill or skillet. Place bread on a clean, flat, and dry work surface. Spread Brie in a thick, even layer on bread, then top with sliced apples, Havarti cheese, and the top half of sandwich. Butter both sides of sandwich and grill until browned and crisp and cheese is melted, about 10 minutes if using panini grill and 7 minutes per side if using skillet.

Remove and repeat process with remaining ingredients to make additional sandwiches.

Keep grilled sandwiches warm in 200°F (90°C) oven. Pull apart sandwiches and insert baby spinach and salami. Close, slice, and serve warm.

2 lb (1 kg) medium asparagus, ends trimmed, stalks peeled, and cut in half lengthwise

1 large Vidalia or sweet yellow onion, peeled, cut in half, and thinly sliced

3 tablespoons (45 ml) extra-virgin olive oil, plus extra for brushing

2 tablespoons (28 g) unsalted butter

2 teaspoons (5 g) grated lemon peel

1/4 cup (60 ml) fresh-squeezed lemon juice

salt

coarse ground black pepper

4 fresh tarragon sprigs, stems removed and leaves chopped

12 slices crusty ciabatta bread or other crusty loaf

1/4 lb (115 g) prosciutto, thinly sliced

6 ounces (170 g) Gruyere cheese, sliced

6 slices Swiss cheese

Preheat the oven to 450°F (230°C). Place the asparagus and onions on a large baking sheet, drizzle with olive oil, dot with butter, sprinkle with lemon zest and lemon juice, and season with salt and pepper. Toss the vegetables lightly to distribute the seasonings. Bake until soft and just starting to brown, about 20 minutes. Remove from oven, transfer to a bowl, toss with tarragon, then set aside.

Preheat panini grill or skillet. Place bread on a flat, clean, and dry work surface, then top with Gruyere, Swiss, and remaining slice of bread. Brush the top with olive oil and transfer to hot grill or pan, oiled side down; brush remaining side with olive oil. Grill until cheese is melted and bread is browned and crisp, about 10 minutes if using panini grill or 7 minutes per side if using skillet. If using skillet, place a heavier skillet or stone on the sandwich to weigh it down while it cooks.

Repeat process with remaining ingredients to make additional sandwiches.

Keep grilled sandwiches warm in a 200°F (90°C) oven. Pull sandwiches apart and insert prosciutto and asparagus and onion mixture. Close sandwiches, slice, and serve.

[Makes 6 sandwiches]

Roasted Asparagus and Sweet Onion Panini with Gruyere

Asparagus is one of my favorite vegetables, and whether it's grilled, sautéed, or roasted, it has a wonderfully unique flavor. Roasting it with onions is one way to concentrate and mix the flavors of both vegetables.

chapter 3

Cold Sandwiches, Wraps, Pitas, **and More**

An American Hero

Depending on where you live, this sandwich could be called a sub, grinder, po'boy, hoagie, wedge, muffaletta, or zepplin. Whatever the regional name, you have to be a "hero" to finish it, which explains the origin of this sandwich's name, according to Clementine Paddleford, a *New York Herald Tribune* food writer from the 1930s.

½ cup (120 ml) Roasted Garlic Aioli (see recipe, page 111)

¼ cup (16 g) thinly sliced basil

½ teaspoon (1 g) coarse ground black pepper

2 scallions, minced

1 (16-ounce [455 g]) loaf italian or french bread, sliced in half horizontally

2 teaspoons (10 ml) balsamic vinegar

2 teaspoons (10 ml) extra-virgin olive oil

¼ lb (115 g) thinly sliced deli prosciutto

¼ lb (115 g) thinly sliced genoa salami

¼ lb (115 g) sliced white american cheese

¼ lb (115 g) thinly sliced large pepperoni rounds

¼ lb (115 g) thinly sliced sweet capicola

¼ lb (115 g) honey-roasted deli ham

¼ lb (115 g) sliced provolone cheese

1 small yellow pepper, thinly sliced

2 large vine-ripened tomatoes, thinly sliced

1 red onion, thinly sliced

1 cup (60 g) shredded iceberg lettuce

Combine garlic aioli, basil, black pepper, and scallions in a small bowl. Lay out the bread cut side up, then drizzle each side with balsamic vinegar and olive oil just to flavor; do not saturate the bread. Spread each half generously with garlic aioli mixture. Layer on the meats and cheeses, folding the slices if necessary to fit on the bread, then top with peppers, tomatoes, onions, and lettuce. Close sandwich, press firmly to push ingredients together, slice in 2" (5 cm)-wide strips, and serve.

[For the coleslaw]
Combine cabbage, carrots, red onion, and apple in a large bowl. In a separate bowl, combine aioli, mustard, cider vinegar, lemon juice, and sugar. Pour this dressing over the cabbage mixture and toss to thoroughly combine. Season slaw with celery seed, onion powder, salt, and back pepper. Chill for at least 2 hours before serving.

1 lb (455 g) fresh lobster meat

½ cup (120 ml) mayonnaise

2 tablespoons (8 g) fresh chopped tarragon

salt

coarse ground black pepper

8 slices smoked bacon, cooked

8 leaves Bibb lettuce

2 medium fresh tomatoes, thinly sliced

1 avocado, thinly sliced

juice of two lemons

white bread, sliced thick

Place lobster meat, mayonnaise, tarragon, 1 tablespoon (15 ml) lemon juice, ¼ teaspoon (1.5 g) salt, and ¼ teaspoon (.5 g) pepper in a bowl and toss to combine. Toss avocado with remaining lemon juice to prevent browning. Lay out bread on clean, flat, and dry work surface, then layer with 1 lettuce leaf, a quarter of the lobster salad, 2 slices bacon, 2 slices tomato, and 4 slices avocado. Add second slice of bread and press down slightly. Repeat process with remaining ingredients to make additional sandwiches. Cut in half and serve.

[Makes 4 sandwiches]

Lobster Salad BLT

To many in New England, summer and lobster salad go hand in hand. The trick to lobster salad is to not outshine the lobster: a few choice ingredients will go a long way. Here, I have paired the salad with crisp, smoky bacon, giving the classic BLT a New England twist. If you prefer to omit the bacon, the salad is great on its own.

4 (8-ounce [225g]) skinless chicken breasts

1/4 cup (60 ml) orange juice

2 tablespoons (40 g) honey

2 tablespoons (3 g) chopped fresh rosemary

3 tablespoons (45 ml) olive oil

1 teaspoon (2 g) coarse ground black pepper

2 tablespoons (30 ml) balsamic vinegar

1/2 teaspoon (3 g) kosher salt

2 cups (300 g) green grapes, sliced in half

1/4 cup (40 g) crumbled Gorgonzola cheese

1 medium fennel bulb, sliced thin

1/2 cup (60 g) chopped, toasted walnuts

1 cup (235 ml) Champagne Grape Vinaigrette (recipe follows)

6 leaves Bibb lettuce (in the shape of a cup)

CHAMPAGNE GRAPE VINAIGRETTE:

Makes about 1 cup (235 ml)

1/2 cup (120 ml) orange juice

1/4 cup (60 ml) Champagne vinegar

2 shallots, minced

1 tablespoon (4 g) chopped fresh mint

1 teaspoon (5 g) sugar

1 tablespoon (15 g) Dijon mustard

1/4 cup (60 ml) grapeseed oil

[Makes 6 sandwiches]

Roasted Chicken Salad with Green Grapes and Walnuts

In early summer, green grapes are perfectly ripe and delicious, and combining them with chicken and walnuts makes a perfect summer afternoon lunch. Though not technically a sandwich, this salad is perfect on its own, on a bed of leafy greens, or on a toasted croissant.

Preheat oven to 400°F (200°C). Combine orange juice, honey, and rosemary in a mixing bowl and whisk to combine. Gradually add olive oil in a steady stream while whisking to emulsify, then season with salt and pepper. Place the chicken in a baking dish, skin side down, and rub generously with olive oil mixture. Bake until browned and cooked through (the internal temperature should reach 165°F [75°C]), about 45 minutes. Remove and let cool. When cool enough to handle, pull the chicken meat from the bones in fine strips and set aside.

Meanwhile, combine grapes, Gorgonzola, fennel, walnuts, and Champagne Grape Vinaigrette in large mixing bowl and toss to combine. Add chicken and toss, then cover and refrigerate for at least 1 hour. Serve in lettuce cup on individual plates with a toasted croissant.

[For champagne grape vinaigrette]

Combine all ingredients except for the grape seed oil in the bowl of a food processor fitted with the blade attachment and pulse to chop. With the motor running, gradually add the grape seed oil in a steady stream to emulsify. Once thickened, season with salt and pepper and refrigerate for at least 30 minutes.

2 cups (475 ml) prepared garlic hummus

1 small english cucumber, sliced into 3" (7.5 cm) lengths, then thinly sliced lengthwise

1 medium red onion, thinly sliced

1 large roasted red pepper, seeded and sliced (see recipe, page 28)

1 large roasted yellow pepper, seeded and sliced (see recipe, page 28)

1 cup (50 g) alfalfa sprouts

4 leaves Bibb lettuce

½ cup (120 ml) Feta Pine Nut Spread (recipe follows)

4 bagels, plain or favorite variety, sliced horizontally and toasted

2 tablespoons (28 g) butter, room temperature

FETA PINE NUT SPREAD:

Makes about 1½ cups (355 ml)

4 ounces (115 g) cream cheese, softened

1 tablespoon (28 g) mayonnaise

¼ cup (40 g) feta cheese, crumbled

¼ cup (35 g) pine nuts, toasted

½ teaspoon (.5 g) dried oregano

Preheat oven broiler. Slice bagels in half horizontally, spread inside of each half evenly with butter, and toast under broiler until brown, about 3 minutes. Remove from oven and let cool. Spread Feta Pine Nut Spread evenly on the bottom of bagel, then layer with lettuce, cucumber, hummus, red onion, alfalfa sprouts, and roasted red and yellow peppers, divided equally among 4 sandwiches. Spread top half of bagel with remaining spread on and add to sandwich. Repeat process with remaining ingredients to make additional sandwiches. Slice in half and serve.

[For feta pine nut spread]
Combine all ingredients in the bowl of a food processor fitted with the blade attachment. Process until well combined and pine nuts are finely chopped. Remove and refrigerate until ready to use.

[Makes 4 sandwiches]

California Bagel Sandwich

Anytime one thinks of a "California"-style sandwich, the term healthy comes to mind, and this bagel delivers on that promise with hummus; fresh, crisp vegetables; and Feta Pine Nut Spread.

Six 4-ounce (115 g) fresh salmon fillets

olive oil

salt and coarse ground black pepper

6 french baguette rolls

⅓ cup (75 g) Lemon-Dill Mayonnaise (recipe follows)

6 leaves red leaf lettuce

2 large tomatoes, thinly sliced

12 slices smoked bacon, cooked

LEMON-DILL MAYONNAISE:

½ cup (112 g) good-quality mayonnaise

1 teaspoon (5 ml) fresh lemon juice

2 teaspoons (1.5 g) chopped fresh dill

salt and coarse ground black pepper

[Makes 6 sandwiches]

Grilled Salmon and Pepper-Smoked Bacon Club

Salmon is the perfect, meaty fish for grilling. Serve warm or cool in this excellent summertime sandwich. Packing this one for a picnic is a great idea; just serve the Lemon-Dill Mayonnaise on the side.

Preheat outdoor grill or stovetop grill pan to medium-high heat. Trim salmon fillets of any fatty pieces. Rub with olive oil and season with salt and black pepper. Grill salmon, skin side down first, for about 6 minutes on each side, until pink and meat begins to flake. Remove from grill and set aside. Slice baguettes open lengthwise, being careful not to slice all the way through. Spread Lemon-Dill Mayonnaise on bread and top with a leaf of lettuce. Place sliced tomato on lettuce, follow with grilled salmon fillet, and finish with two slices of cooked smoked bacon. Serve.

[For the lemon-dill mayonnaise]
Combine all ingredients in a small mixing bowl. Refrigerate until ready to use.

SPICY DRY RUB:

3 tablespoons (28 g) paprika

2 tablespoons (4 g) ground cumin

1 tablespoon (9 g) garlic powder

2 tablespoons (28 g) packed brown sugar

1 tablespoon (6 g) dry mustard

3 tablespoons (12 g) dried oregano

3 tablespoons (54 g) coarse salt

2 teaspoons (4 g) coarse ground black pepper

1 (5- to 7-lb [2.3 to 3.2 kg]) pork roast, pork shoulder, or Boston butt

CIDER-MUSTARD BARBECUE SAUCE:

1½ cups (355 ml) brown mustard

½ cup (120 ml) ketchup

1 cup (235 ml) cider vinegar

½ cup (120 ml) apple cider

2 tablespoons (30 ml) Worcestershire sauce

⅓ cup (75 g) packed light brown sugar

1 teaspoon (2 g) cayenne pepper

1 teaspoon (6 g) kosher salt

1 teaspoon (2 g) coarse ground black pepper

6 pita rounds, cut in half and opened

1 recipe Coleslaw (recipe follows)

COLESLAW:

1 head green cabbage, shredded

2 large carrots, grated on the large grate of a box grater

1 red onion, thinly sliced

1 green apple, peeled, shredded, and tossed in lemon juice

1½ cups (355 ml) Roasted Garlic Aioli (see recipe, page 111) or prepared mayonnaise

¼ cup (60 g) Dijon mustard

1 tablespoon (15 ml) cider vinegar

Juice of one lemon

1 teaspoon (5 g) sugar

½ teaspoon (2 g) celery seed

½ teaspoon (1.5 g) onion powder

salt

coarse ground black pepper

Combine paprika, cumin, garlic powder, brown sugar, dry mustard, oregano, salt, and black pepper in a small bowl. Rub the spice mixture all over the pork, covering the roast thoroughly and working the rub into the meat with your hands. Cover and refrigerate for at least 1 hour or overnight. Preheat oven to 300°F (150°C). Place the pork in a roasting pan, uncovered, and roast for about 4 hours, until meat is tender and falling apart, or internal temperature reads 170°F (75°C). Combine brown mustard, ketchup, vinegar, cider, Worcestershire sauce, brown sugar, cayenne, salt, and black pepper in a small saucepan, then simmer over medium heat until sugar is dissolved, about 10 minutes. Remove from heat and set aside. Remove pork from oven, cover with foil, and let sit about 15 minutes. While still warm, pull the pork into strips using a fork. Place shredded pork in a bowl and toss with 1½ cups (355 ml) of the sauce. To serve, open pockets, spoon pork into pita, top with coleslaw, and serve with remaining sauce on the side.

[Makes 12 sandwiches]

Barbecued Pulled Pork and Coleslaw Pocket

Pulled pork, a Southern favorite, is served either on a bun, like a sandwich, or piled on a plate with baked beans. In this recipe, I have made what's usually a messy, saucy concoction a little neater by serving it in a pita pocket.

1 (6-ounce [170 g]) package Asian soba noodles

1 tablespoon (15 ml) toasted sesame oil

1 (8-ounce [235 ml]) jar Thai peanut sauce

1/4 cup (64 g) creamy peanut butter

2 tablespoons (15 g) toasted sesame seeds

3 tablespoons (45 ml) soy sauce

2 tablespoons (40 g) honey

1 tablespoon (9 g) brown sugar

1/4 cup (60 ml) orange juice

1/4 cup (60 ml) peach nectar

1 tablespoon (15 ml) fresh lime juice

2 cups (450 g) roasted, shredded chicken breast meat

1 medium red pepper, thinly sliced

1 cup (120 g) julienned carrot

1 small english cucumber, thinly sliced on the diagonal

2 scallions, sliced into 2" (5 cm) pieces, then thinly sliced lengthwise

1/2 cup (75 g) roasted, salted peanuts, coarsely chopped

1/4 cup (5 g) coarsely chopped fresh cilantro

6 chili wraps

Bring a large pot of salted water to a boil. Add soba noodles and cook according to package instructions. Transfer to colander under running cold water and drain, then place in medium mixing bowl, toss with sesame oil, and let cool. In a large mixing bowl, combine Thai peanut sauce, peanut butter, sesame seeds, soy sauce, honey, brown sugar, orange juice, peach nectar, and lime juice; then set aside.

Toss shredded chicken with 1 cup (235 ml) of the peanut sauce mixture in a medium-size mixing bowl, then set aside. Add noodles, red pepper, carrot, cucumber, scallions, peanuts, and cilantro to the remaining peanut sauce. Toss to combine and coat thoroughly, then add chicken and combine. Lay wraps out on a clean, dry, and flat surface, place a generous portion of noodle salad in the center of each wrap, fold in the sides, and roll up tightly. Cut in half on the diagonal and serve.

[Makes 6 sandwiches]

Thai Peanut Chicken Wrap

Peanut sauce is a great flavor with chicken and noodles. Add the crunch of fresh vegetables and roasted peanuts to make this wrap a lunchtime hit.

MARINADE:

½ cup (120 ml) soy sauce

¼ cup (60 ml) orange juice

3 tablespoons (60 g) honey

¼ cup (55 g) packed
brown sugar

2 tablespoons (30 ml)
scotch whiskey

3 tablespoons (45 ml) hoisin sauce

1 tablespoon (10 g) grated
fresh ginger

1 teaspoon (5 g) chinese
five-spice powder

1 teaspoon (6 g) salt

1 tablespoon (6 g) coarse
ground black pepper

2 tablespoons (30 ml)
toasted sesame oil

2 tablespoons (30 ml) vegetable oil

2 pork tenderloins
(about 2½ lb [1 kg])

8 red pepper or rice paper wraps

2 cups (60 g) shredded Bibb lettuce

1 cup (120 g) shredded carrots

4 scallions, thinly sliced on
the diagonal

⅓ cup (20 g) fresh
cilantro leaves

½ cup (75 g) chopped,
dry-roasted peanuts (optional)

⅓ cup (75 ml) Asian Lime
Vinaigrette (recipe follows)

ASIAN LIME VINAIGRETTE:

Makes about 2 cups (475 ml)

1 clove garlic, finely minced

1 fresh red chili pepper, seeds and stem removed and minced

1/4 cup (60 ml) sugar

1/4 cup (60 ml) lime juice, including pulp

5 tablespoons (75 ml) Thai fish sauce

1/2 cup (120 ml) water

1 cup (235 ml) olive oil

1/4 cup (5 g) chopped fresh cilantro

To prepare the marinade, combine the first ten ingredients in a mixing bowl and whisk to combine. While whisking, gradually add sesame and vegetable oils in a thin, steady stream. Add pork tenderloins, toss to coat, then cover and refrigerate for at least 1 hour. Preheat outdoor grill or stovetop grill pan to medium-high. Remove pork from refrigerator and let come to room temperature. Place on grill and sear all around, about 4 minutes on each side, then reduce heat to medium-low and cook until internal temperature reaches 125°F (50°C), turning periodically to cook evenly. Remove from heat and let sit 10 minutes, then slice into thin strips. Lay out wrap on a clean, dry, and flat work surface. If using rice paper, dampen with a cloth until tender and pliable, then lay out flat. Layer wrap with lettuce, carrots, scallions, pork, cilantro leaves, and peanuts, then drizzle with Asian Lime Vinaigrette. Roll wrap one-quarter turn, then fold in sides and continue to roll up. Repeat process with remaining ingredients to make additional wraps. Slice in half on the diagonal and serve. Extra vinaigrette can be served on the side.

[For asian lime vinaigrette]
Combine garlic, chili pepper, and sugar in a small bowl, then use a fork to mash together and form a paste. Add lime juice and pulp, fish sauce, and water, then stir to dissolve the sugar. Strain the sauce, then whisk with olive oil to thicken, and add cilantro. Cover and refrigerate until ready to use. The dressing can be covered and refrigerated for up to 1 week.

[Makes 8 wraps]

Asian Pork Tenderloin Wraps

This sandwich features crisp, garden fresh vegetables and a drizzle of Asian Lime Vinaigrette, both of which complement the robust grilled pork very well.

2 ears fresh corn, cleaned

2 tablespoons (28 g) butter

2 tablespoons (20 g) fresh, chopped garlic

salt

black pepper

1 teaspoon (1 g) fresh chopped flat-leaf parsley

1 teaspoon (1 g) fresh chopped cilantro

2 tablespoons (15 g) chopped red pepper

2 tablespoons (15 g) chopped red onion

1 tablespoon (15 ml) red wine vinegar

Juice from one lime

6 tomato wraps

4 ounces (115 g) pepper Jack cheese, thinly sliced

4 ounces (115 g) Muenster cheese, thinly sliced

6 leaves red leaf lettuce

1 avocado, thinly sliced

Chipotle Spread (recipe follows)

1 lb (455 g) smoked deli turkey breast, thinly sliced

FOR CHIPOTLE SPREAD:

Makes about 1/2 cup (120 ml)

1 tablespoon (7 g) cream cheese, softened

2 tablespoons (55 g) mayonnaise

2 tablespoons (28 g) sour cream

1 teaspoon (5 ml) red wine vinegar

1 chipotle pepper in adobo sauce, seeded and chopped fine

Preheat grill to high. Place corn cob on piece of heavy-duty aluminum foil and top with butter, garlic, salt, and pepper. Wrap corn tightly, then grill for 20 minutes, turning occasionally. Remove, unwrap, and let cool. When cool enough to handle, cut kernels from cob into a mixing bowl and remove any strings. Combine with parsley, cilantro, red pepper, red onion, vinegar, and lime juice, then refrigerate for at least 30 minutes.

Lay out wrap on flat, clean, and dry work surface, and layer with cheeses, lettuce, corn relish, and avocado; drizzle with Chipotle Spread, and top with turkey. Repeat process with remaining ingredients to make additional wraps. Serve.

[For chipotle spread]
Combine all ingredients in a small mixing bowl, cover and refrigerate for at least 30 minutes.

[Makes 6 sandwiches]

Border Turkey Wrap

When you think of border cuisine, hot and spicy comes to mind, and chipotle peppers fit the bill with flavorful abandon. Generally available canned in an adobo sauce, chipotle peppers pack quite a punch—be careful not to overdo it. Combined with crisp, fresh vegetables and roasted turkey breast, the peppers find a great home in this south-of-the-border wrap.

8 slices white bread

¼ cup (55 g) mayonnaise

6 leaves green lettuce, torn

12 slices peppered bacon, cooked

8 ounces (225 g) dill Havarti cheese, sliced

4 slices pumpernickel bread

¼ cup (60 g) Coleman's prepared mustard

3 plum tomatoes, thinly sliced

1½ lb (680 g) deli roast beef, sliced thin

Lay out 4 slices of white bread on a clean, dry, and flat surface. Spread each slice of bread evenly with half of the mayonnaise. Layer bread with half of the lettuce, bacon, and Havarti cheese, then top with pumpernickel bread. Spread mustard evenly over pumpernickel and top with remaining lettuce, tomato, and roast beef. Spread remaining pieces of white bread with remaining mayonnaise and place on top of sandwich, mayonnaise side down. Place a long pick or skewer in the center of all four quarters of the sandwich. Cut diagonal criss-cross cuts and serve.

[Makes 4 sandwiches]

Black and White Club

The flavor combination here is great, but the real treat is the play of colors in the layers of pumpernickel and white bread. Sliced and served in wedges, this sandwich is especially appropriate for lunchtime.

Jerked Chicken Breast Sandwich with Grilled Plantain, Sliced Mango, and Coconut Cilantro Spread

Jerked chicken is an easy way to pack a punch into any sandwich. Choose from numerous jerked seasonings available in the spice aisle or marinade section of your local supermarket, or use your own time-tested favorite. Don't be afraid to spice it up—the Coconut Cilantro Spread will cool it down.

4 (4-ounce [115 g]) boneless, skinless chicken breasts

3 tablespoons (45 ml) olive oil

¼ cup (60 g) Jamaican jerk seasoning

1 tablespoon (20 g) honey

2 ripe plantains

1 mango, peeled, cored, and thinly sliced

8 slices large peasant bread

⅓ cup (75 ml) Coconut Cilantro Spread (recipe follows)

COCONUT CILANTRO SPREAD:

Makes about ½ cup (120 ml)

¼ cup (60 ml) Thai coconut sauce

¼ cup (16 g) fresh cilantro leaves, coarsely chopped

2 tablespoons (30 ml) lime juice

Place chicken in a bowl and add olive oil, jerk seasoning, and honey. Marinate for at least 1 hour. Peel plantains and cut into ¼-inch (0.6 cm) -thick slices on the diagonal. Coat slices with olive oil and set aside. Preheat grill to high, then reduce heat to medium-high. Grill chicken until cooked through, about 7 minutes per side. Remove and let cool for about 5 minutes. Slice thinly, cutting with the grain of the meat. Grill plantain slices until golden and tender, about 3 minutes per side. Lay out bread slices and spread evenly with Coconut Cilantro Spread, then layer chicken, plantains, and mango. Add second slice of bread, slice in half, and serve.

[For coconut cilantro spread] Combine all ingredients in a small mixing bowl, cover, and refrigerate for at least 30 minutes.

Sandwiches, Panini, and Wraps

4 large spinach wraps

4 ounces (50 g) Yogurt Dill Spread (recipe follows)

4 ounces (115 g) fresh baby spinach or arugula

1 english cucumber, thinly sliced on a diagonal

2 vine-ripened tomatoes, thinly sliced

2 fresh avocados, peeled and thinly sliced

YOGURT DILL SPREAD:

Makes about ⅓ cup (80 g)

1 teaspoon (.5 g) fresh chopped dill

1 teaspoon (5 ml) fresh lemon juice

⅓ cup (75 ml) plain yogurt

1 tablespoon (14 g) light sour cream

1 teaspoon (5 g) sugar

salt

coarse ground black pepper

Lay out spinach wrap on clean, dry, flat surface. Coat the center with 2 tablespoons (30 g) Yogurt Dill Spread. Layer with spinach, cucumber, tomatoes, and avocado slices. Fold in sides of wrap to meet the filling and then roll. Repeat process with remaining ingredients to make additional wraps. Cut in half diagonally and serve. Can be made up to 1 hour in advance and refrigerated until ready to slice and serve.

[For yogurt dill spread]
Combine all ingredients in small mixing bowl and refrigerate for at least 30 minutes

[Makes 4 sandwiches]

Avocado and Cucumber Wrap

For the vegetable lover, avocado and cucumbers together are delightful. The crisp, fresh taste of cucumbers, paired with the smooth texture of avocados is a perfect partnership. Add a creamy, cold yogurt dill spread, and this wrap bursts with flavor; it's a healthy choice for any meal.

1 gallon (3.5 l) water

2 tablespoons (2.5 g) McCormick Old Bay seasoning

3 lemons, thinly sliced

1 teaspoon (1.5 g) black peppercorns

2 bay leaves

1½ lbs (680 g) small shrimp, tails removed, peeled, and deveined

½ cup (112 g) Hellmann's mayonnaise

¾ cup (90 g) chopped celery, patted dry

1 tablespoon (15 ml) fresh lemon juice

1 garlic clove, minced

2 tablespoons (13 g) finely chopped scallions

¼ cup (30 g) sliced almonds, toasted

2 tablespoons (8 g) fresh tarragon, chopped

½ teaspoon (3 g) salt

¼ teaspoon (.5 g) freshly ground black pepper

2 tablespoons (28 g) butter, room temperature

4 large butter croissants, sliced in half horizontally

Bring water, Old Bay seasoning, lemon slices, peppercorns, and bay leaves to a boil in a large stock pot over high heat. Add shrimp and cook for 1 minute. Turn off the heat, stir, and allow shrimp to sit in the hot water for 3 to 4 minutes, or until fully cooked. Transfer shrimp from stock pot to a strainer and rinse well under cold water. Wrap shrimp in clean, dry towel and refrigerate for several hours. (It is important that the shrimp be thoroughly dry and cold for the sandwich preparation.) Combine mayonnaise, celery, lemon juice, garlic, scallions, almonds, tarragon, salt, and pepper in a medium bowl. Stir to combine, then add shrimp and toss to incorporate. Refrigerate salad for at least an hour.

Preheat broiler or toaster oven. Spread inside of croissant half with butter, then toast under broiler or in toaster oven until golden brown, about 3 minutes. Let cool 2 to 3 minutes. Layer with watercress, shrimp salad, and croissant top. Repeat process with remaining ingredients to make additional sandwiches. Slice in half and serve.

[Makes 4 sandwiches]

Tarragon Shrimp Salad on Toasted Croissant

Fresh tarragon adds a subtle, exquisite flavor to shrimp salad. Be sure to let the salad refrigerate for at least an hour to really let the flavors marry. Serve the salad atop a bed of mixed salad greens for lower-fat option.

1 zucchini, thinly sliced lengthwise

1 summer squash, thinly sliced lengthwise

2 large carrots, peeled and thickly sliced on the diagonal

1/4 cup (60 ml) extra-virgin olive oil

kosher salt

coarse ground black pepper

2 avocados, peeled and thinly sliced

juice of one lemon

8 whole wheat or other flavor wraps

1 (12-ounce [340 g]) container hummus

8 leaves green or red leaf lettuce

1 english cucumber, thinly sliced on the diagonal

4 ounces (115 g) alfalfa sprouts

1 head radicchio, sliced in half and then into thin strips (optional)

8 ounces (225 g) favorite bottled ranch-style dressing

[Makes 8 wraps]

Grilled Spring Vegetable Wrap

Top this vegetable sandwich with cool ranch dressing.

Preheat outdoor grill, electric grill, or stovetop grill pan to medium-high heat. In a large bowl, toss zucchini, summer squash, and carrot slices with olive oil. Sprinkle with salt and black pepper. Grill the vegetables about 3 minutes per side, until tender and browned. The carrots may take a bit longer than the other vegetables, depending on the thickness of the slices. Remove vegetables from grill and set aside to cool.

Meanwhile, slice the avocado into thin strips and sprinkle with lemon juice, salt, and pepper; set aside until assembly. For assembly, lay one whole wheat wrap on a flat, clean, and dry surface. Spread hummus in an even layer on the wrap, leaving a 1 inch (2.5 cm) border around the edges of the wrap. Layer with one lettuce leaf, followed by even amounts of the grilled vegetables, cucumber, and avocado, and finishing with radicchio and alfalfa sprouts. Top the vegetables with 2 tablespoons (30 g) of ranch-style dressing. Fold the left and right sides in and over the other fold and roll the wrap. Slice wrap diagonally in half and serve.

½ cup (115 ml) mayonnaise

1 tablespoon (15 g) Dijon mustard

¼ cup (20 g) apple cider jelly or apple jam

2 scallions, finely chopped

⅓ cup (40 g) chopped celery

1 green apple, peeled, cored, and finely chopped

¾ cup (90 g) chopped, toasted pecans

2 teaspoons (2 g) chopped, fresh Italian flat-leaf parsley

1½ lb (680 g) boneless, skinless chicken breasts, cooked and thinly sliced

salt

coarsely ground black pepper

16 slices multigrain bread, or favorite bread or croissant

Leafy greens

Combine mayonnaise, mustard, jelly, scallions, celery, apple, pecans, and parsley in a large mixing bowl, and stir to combine thoroughly. Add chicken, toss to coat, and season with salt and pepper. Cover and refrigerate for at least one hour. Serve atop mixed leafy greens, such as a mesculun mix, or a combination of arugula, radicchio, and romaine lettuce, or serve on toasted bread as a sandwich.

[Makes 4 sandwiches]

Apple Cider Chicken Salad Sandwich

Chicken salad is probably one of the most popular sandwich fillings out there. The autumn flavors of crisp apples and cider jam make this chicken salad unique. This recipe, which makes about 4 cups (925 ml), can also be used atop a green salad.

Roast Chicken Sandwich **with** Balsamic Cranberry Relish

The cranberry relish in this recipe doesn't have to be limited to just this sandwich. Its vibrant flavor goes great with roast pork or a stuffed turkey breast. Canned cranberry sauce makes available all year long what is typically saved for a day at Thanksgiving. Enjoy this sandwich any time of year.

1 (16-ounce [455 g]) can whole-berry cranberry sauce

1 teaspoon (5 g) lemon zest

¼ cup (60 ml) balsamic vinegar

¼ cup (30 g) chopped pecans, toasted

1 tablespoon (14 g) packed brown sugar

¼ teaspoon (1.5 g) salt

½ teaspoon (1 g) coarse ground black pepper

8 slices multigrain bread, thickly sliced

4 teaspoons (20 ml) Coleman's prepared mustard (optional)

4 leaves Bibb lettuce

1 Anjou or Bosc pear, peeled and thinly sliced

8 slices peppered thick-cut bacon, cooked

2 lb (1 kg) deli-roasted chicken, thinly sliced

[cranberry relish]
Combine cranberry sauce, lemon zest, balsamic vinegar, pecans, brown sugar, salt, and black pepper in a medium-sized saucepan over medium heat. Bring mixture to a boil, reduce heat to low, and simmer for about 15 minutes until thickened. Remove from heat and let cool, then cover and refrigerate until ready to use. The cranberry relish can be served chilled or warm.

Lay out 4 slices of bread on a clean, dry, and flat work surface. Spread ½ teaspoon (5 ml) mustard on each slice of bread. Dividing ingredients evenly among sandwiches, top with lettuce, cranberry relish, pears, bacon, and chicken. Spread top slice of bread with remaining mustard and place on sandwich. Slice and serve.

6 italian hoagie rolls

6 (6-ounce [170 g]) catfish fillets

4 cups (440 g) all-purpose flour

2 tablespoons (9 g)
baking powder

1 teaspoon (2 g) ground
red pepper

2 teaspoons (12 g) kosher salt

2 teaspoons (4 g)
coarse ground black pepper

4 (12-ounce [355 ml]) bottles
dark beer

Vegetable oil for frying

SWEET CABBAGE SLAW:

2 cups (180 g) thinly sliced
red cabbage

1 small red onion,
cut in half and thinly sliced

2 carrots, finely shredded

1 head belgian endive, thinly
sliced

1 teaspoon (1 g) chopped
fresh italian flat-leaf parsley

1/4 cup (60 ml) cider vinegar

2 tablespoons (30 g) mayonnaise

1 tablespoon (15 g)
honey-Dijon mustard

2 tablespoons (12 g)
chopped shallots

1 clove fresh garlic, minced

1 tablespoon (18 g) brown sugar

1/4 cup (15 g) packed
chopped fresh basil

1/2 cup (120 ml) olive oil

salt

black pepper

HORSERADISH REMOULADE:

1/4 cup (60 g) mayonnaise

1 teaspoon (5 g) Dijon mustard

2 teaspoons (10 ml) minced
cornichons or sour gherkins

1 1/2 teaspoons (8 g) minced capers

2 cloves garlic, minced

1 tablespoon (15 g) horseradish

1 teaspoon (1 g) fresh chopped
italian flat-leaf parsley

3 dashes hot pepper sauce

Combine flour, baking powder,
red pepper, salt, and pepper in
a large mixing bowl. Add beer,
then whisk until smooth. Cover
and chill 1 hour.

[sweet cabbage slaw]
Place cabbage, onion, carrots,
endive, and parsley in a mixing
bowl. Combine cider vinegar,
mayonnaise, mustard, shallots,
garlic, brown sugar, and basil in

[Makes 6 sandwiches]

Batter-Fried Catfish Hoagie with Sweet Cabbage Slaw and Horseradish Remoulade

In the South, where I grew up, catfish is plentiful and delicious. A typical southern beer batter blankets these flavorful fillets for an outstanding summer sandwich.

a blender and puree. With blender running, add the olive oil in a steady stream to emulsify. Remove from blender and season with salt and pepper. Pour dressing over cabbage mixture and toss to combine. Refrigerate at least 1 hour. Combine all ingredients for Horseradish Remoulade in a small mixing bowl and stir to combine. Cover and refrigerate

at least 30 minutes.

Pour vegetable oil to a depth of 1½ inches (3.8 cm) in a heavy skillet, then heat to 375°F (190°C). Sprinkle catfish fillets with salt and pepper. Dip fish in batter, coating both sides generously; hold over bowl of batter and let excess drip back into bowl. Add to skillet and fry, two fillets at a time, until golden, 1½ to 2 minutes per

side. When done, place on paper towel to drain. Repeat process with remaining fillets.

Slice hoagie horizontally, three-quarters of the way through. Open and spread both sides with Horseradish Remoulade. Place catfish on bottom half of sandwich and top with ¼ cup (60 ml) Sweet Cabbage Slaw. Repeat process with remaining ingredients to make additional sandwiches. Serve.

[For frying fish fillets]
When placing the battered fish fillet into the hot oil, hold one end of the fillet between the finger tips of one hand. Start at the back of the skillet and slowly dip the free end of the fillet into the oil. Then gently lay the fillet into the oil. **Never** drop the fillets into the oil or the moisture inside will cause the hot oil to bubble and splash.

Sandwiches, Panini, and Wraps

12 slices whole wheat or other favorite bread

3 (6-ounce [170 g]) boneless, skinless chicken breasts

½ cup (120 ml) orange juice

½ cup (118 ml) ginger ale or sweet, clear soda

1 teaspoon (2 g) black pepper

1 tablespoon (2 g) chopped fresh rosemary

1 tablespoon (4 g) chopped fresh flat-leaf parsley

1 tablespoon (15 ml) Worcestershire sauce

¼ cup (60 ml) extra-virgin olive oil

6 slices smoked bacon, cooked

6 leaves green lettuce, torn

6 ounces (170 g) Monterey Jack cheese, sliced

2 vine-ripened tomatoes, thinly sliced

¼ cup (112 g) Tarraggon Mayonnaise (see recipe, page 109)

Combine orange juice, ginger ale, pepper, rosemary, parsley, and Worcestershire sauce in a mixing bowl; whisk in olive oil in a steady stream to emulsify. Add chicken and refrigerate for at least 1 hour or up to 2 days.

Preheat oven broiler or toaster oven. Butter one side of eight bread slices, then place butter side up on sheetpan and toast until browned, about 2 minutes. Remove and let cool. Repeat with remaining bread, toasting both sides.

Preheat grill to high, then grill chicken until browned and cooked through, about 7 minutes per side. Transfer to cutting board and let cool.

When cool enough to handle, slice into thin strips, cutting with the grain. Working on a clean, dry, and flat surface, lay out four slices of single-side toasted bread, toasted side down. Coat each evenly with Tarragon Mayonnaise, then layer with lettuce, bacon, cheese, double-toasted bread, mayonnaise, lettuce, tomato, chicken, and cheese. Spread Tarragon Mayonnaise on untoasted side of remaining slice of bread, then place on top of sandwiches, toasted side up. Place one long toothpick in the center of each sandwich quarter. Cut sandwiches diagonally in half and then in half again and serve.

[Makes 4 sandwiches]

Monterey Chicken Club

A classic club sandwich uses three slices of bread and bacon. This version uses grilled, marinated chicken for a sweet and succulent flavor.

6 (8-ounce [225 g]) boneless, skinless chicken breasts

1½ cups (355 ml) barbecue sauce

1 tablespoon (15 ml) liquid smoke

1 tablespoon (15 ml) Worcestershire sauce

1 tablespoon (20 g) honey

1 tablespoon (10 g) minced fresh garlic

1 tablespoon (6 g) coarse ground black pepper

6 ounces (170 g) smoked Gouda or mozzarella cheese, thinly sliced

1 large red onion, thinly sliced

½ cup (20 g) loosely packed cilantro leaves

6 ciabatta rolls, horizontally sliced

Preheat grill to high. Combine barbecue sauce, liquid smoke, Worcestershire sauce, honey, garlic, and pepper in a large bowl. Set aside half of the sauce mixture. Add chicken to original bowl of sauce mixture, toss to coat, then cover and marinate for at least 30 minutes. Grill chicken on high heat until tender and cooked through, about 7 minutes per side. Remove from grill and set aside. Thinly coat the onions with olive oil and sprinkle with black pepper. Grill on high heat until tender, about 4 minutes on each side. Remove from heat and let cool.

Once chicken is cool enough to handle, pull strips of chicken apart or slice thin and toss in ¼ cup (60 ml) of reserved barbecue sauce. Lay out bottoms of rolls, coat with a thin layer of barbecue sauce. Dividing ingredients evenly among sandwiches, top with cilantro leaves, red onions, chicken, and cheese. Brush inside of top half of rolls with remaining barbecue sauce and top sandwichs. Serve.

[A note about grilling chicken]
The recipes in this book call for you to grill chicken on high heat until cooked through, about 7 minutes per side. However, the cooking time will vary according to the thickness of the chicken and the temperature of the grill. If in doubt, the internal temperature of the cooked chicken should reach at least 165°F (75°C).

[Makes 6 sandwiches]

Barbecue Chicken and Gouda on Ciabatta

Ciabatta bread is the quintessential "panini" bread, yielding beautifully grilled sandwiches. Here, smoked Gouda pairs with hearty barbecued chicken to make a perfect summer treat.

1 medium red pepper

1 medium yellow pepper

1 medium orange pepper

½ cup (120 ml) extra-virgin olive oil, plus extra for brushing peppers

1½ teaspoons (7.5 g) Dijon mustard

1 tablespoon (15 ml) balsamic vinegar

1 tablespoon (4 g) chopped fresh parsley

1 tablespoon (3 g) minced sun-dried tomato

1 teaspoon (4 g) minced fresh garlic

1 teaspoon (6 g) kosher salt

coarse ground black pepper

1 (9" [23 cm]) round loaf focaccia

⅓ cup (75 g) prepared black olive paste

4 ounces (115 g) goat cheese, crumbled

½ medium red onion, thinly sliced (optional)

6 ounces (170 g) marinated artichoke hearts

6 ounces (170 g) prosciutto, thinly sliced

6 ounces (170 g) peppered salami, thinly sliced

4 ounces (115 g) pepperoni, thinly sliced

8 ounces (225 g) fresh buffalo mozzarella cheese, thinly sliced

½ cup (20 g) loosely packed fresh basil leaves

Preheat grill, grill pan, or broiler to high. Rub peppers with olive oil, then place on hot grill and cook until charred, turning frequently so all sides cook evenly, 8 to 10 minutes. Remove from heat and place in a brown paper bag. Seal bag by rolling top and set aside for 5 to 10 minutes. Remove from bag and use fingers to rub charred skin away from flesh. Remove seeds and stems, then slice peppers into 1-inch (2.5 cm) strips and set aside.

Combine mustard, balsamic vinegar, parsley, sun-dried tomato, and garlic in the bowl of a food processor fitted with the blade attachment, and pulse until pureed. With the processor running slowly, add ½ cup (120 ml) olive oil in a steady stream to emulsify. Transfer to bowl, season with salt and pepper, cover, and refrigerate.

Slice focaccia in half horizontally. Remove top and set aside. Drizzle bottom of focaccia with one-third of the vinaigrette, then layer with an even coat of olive paste followed by roasted peppers, goat cheese, red onion, and artichoke hearts. Arrange the mozzarella cheese over the artichoke hearts and layer with prosciutto, salami, and pepperoni. Drizzle with one-third of the vinaigrette and top with basil and chives. Drizzle inside of top half of focaccia with remaining vinaigrette. Place on sandwich, vinaigrette side down.

Wrap sandwich in parchment paper and refrigerate for at least 1 hour before serving. If making sandwich in advance, reserve vinaigrette for dipping or drizzle the insides of the top and bottom of the focaccia just before serving.

[Serves 6 to 8]

Antipasto-Stuffed Focaccia Party Sandwich

This one is big enough to invite the friends over. For the peppers, you can substitute any combination of three colored peppers except green.

2 japanese eggplants, peeled and sliced ¹/₂" (1.3 cm) thick

olive oil for grilling

6 large syrian (pita) breads

1 lb (455 g) shaved roasted leg of lamb or deli roast beef, thinly sliced

8 ounces (225 g) feta cheese, crumbled

¹/₂ cup (16 g) loosely packed italian flat leaf parsley

2 small vine-ripened tomatoes, sliced thin

1 cup (235 ml) Tzatziki Sauce (recipe follows)

TZATZIKI SAUCE:

Makes about 1 cup (235 ml)

¹/₂ cup (50 g) peeled, seeded, and finely chopped cucumber

¹/₂ cup (120 ml) plain yogurt

1 teaspoon (5 ml) olive oil

1 teaspoon (5 ml) lemon juice

¹/₄ teaspoon (1.5 g) kosher salt

¹/₂ teaspoon (.5 g) chopped fresh oregano

1 teaspoon (3 g) minced fresh garlic

1 teaspoon (.3 g) minced fresh dill (optional)

Preheat grill, grill pan, or broiler to high heat. Rub eggplant slices with olive oil and sprinkle with pepper. Grill until golden, about 4 minutes per side. Remove from heat and set aside to cool. Place eggplant slices on one half of pita bread. Top with parsley, shaved lamb or roast beef, feta cheese, and tomatoes. Drizzle with Tzatziki Sauce and fold pita over. Repeat process with remaining ingredients to make additional pitas. Serve.

[For tzatziki sauce]
Combine all ingredients in a bowl, cover, and refrigerate for at least 1 hour.

[Makes 6 wraps]

Folded Greek Syrian with Traditional Tzatziki Sauce

Tzatziki sauce is a traditional Greek complement to lamb sandwiches. I borrowed this wonderful recipe from Emeril Lagasse.

Sandwiches, Panini, and Wraps

1 lb (455 g) fresh lobster meat, chilled and chopped into chunks

½ cup (112 g) good-quality mayonnaise

1 tablespoon (15 g) Dijon mustard

½ cup (50 g) sliced radish

1 tablespoon (4 g) chopped fresh tarragon

kosher salt

coarse ground black pepper

6 hot dog buns, split open

6 tablespoons (90 g) unsalted butter, softened

4 ounces (115 g) fresh arugula, washed and dried

1 yellow or orange pepper, thinly sliced

Combine lobster meat, mayonnaise, mustard, radish, tarragon, salt, and pepper in a large mixing bowl, and stir to combine. Spread butter on inside of hot dog buns and toast under broiler or toaster oven until golden brown, about 3 minutes. Remove and let cool for 2 to 3 minutes. Place arugula on bottom of bun, then top with lobster salad and sliced pepper strips. Repeat process with remaining ingredients to make additional lobster rolls. Serve.

[Makes 6 sandwiches]

New England Lobster Roll

I couldn't write a book on sandwiches without including a traditional New England lobster roll. The key to a delicious lobster roll is not to overwhelm the lobster with a lot of confusing flavors. Simplicity is the key to enjoying the succulent taste of fresh lobster.

1 large loaf rosemary focaccia, or 6 rolls

¼ cup (55 g) Pesto Mayonnaise (recipe follows)

1 cup (60 g) mixed field greens

2 vine-ripened tomatoes, thinly sliced

6 ounces (170 g) fresh mozzarella, thinly sliced

⅓ cup (75 ml) balsamic vinaigrette salad dressing

4 (8-ounce [227 g]) boneless, skinless chicken breasts, grilled and thinly sliced

1 medium red onion, thinly sliced

PESTO MAYONNAISE:

Makes about ⅓ cup (75 g)

⅓ cup (75 g) mayonnaise

1 tablespoon (14 g) sour cream

3 tablespoons (45 ml) favorite basil pesto

½ teaspoon (1 g) coarse ground black pepper

[Serves 6]

Tuscan Chicken on Rosemary Focaccia

When I think of Tuscany, I imagine beautiful, lush countryside, perfect for a spontaneous picnic. This sandwich is best enjoyed with perfectly ripened tomatoes.

Slice open the focaccia loaf horizontally, then generously coat inside of both sides with pesto mayonnaise. Layer bottom half with lettuce, red onion, mozzarella, tomato, and chicken. Drizzle with balsamic vinaigrette and close with top half of roll. Repeat process with remaining ingredients to make additional sandwiches. Serve.

[For pesto mayonnaise]
Combine all ingredients in mixing bowl and stir. Cover and refrigerate for at least 30 minutes.

chapter 4

Condiments and Spreads

Spreads and condiments, I believe, are vital for holding together the ingredients of any good sandwich. Between slices of bread, nestled in wraps, and melted in paninis is a host of flavors and textures that need the binding properties offered by spreads and condiments. If you join me in the belief that all sandwiches deserve a good flavor enhancer in a spread, then I applaud you and offer you the following recipes, any of which can enhance nearly any sandwich, panini, or wrap. I hope that you will try these creations and allow them to stimulate your own ideas for making your own spreads and condiments.

[Makes about 1½ cups (355 ml)]

Black Bean Pesto

Black beans are a healthy way to add flavor and texture to a sandwich spread. In this version of pesto, black beans, cilantro, and peppers combine to create a spread that will kick-start any sandwich.

2 tablespoons (20 g) minced garlic

2 serrano chilies, seeded and minced

1 (14-ounce [397 g]) can black beans, rinsed and drained

1 tablespoon (15 ml) rice vinegar

2 tablespoons (30 ml) olive oil

2 tablespoons (1.5 g) chopped fresh cilantro

1 green onion, chopped

1 tablespoon (7 g) ground cumin

3 drops chipotle pepper sauce (Tabasco sauce or your brand of choice)

Add all ingredients to bowl of food processor fitted with blade attachment. Process until all ingredients are chopped and well combined. Cover and chill until ready to serve.

Lemon-Dill Mayonnaise

To some, a sandwich isn't a sandwich without mayonnaise. For those people, I offer this invigorating alternative to plain mayonnaise.

½ cup (112 g) mayonnaise

1 teaspoon (5 ml) fresh lemon juice

2 teaspoons (1.5 g) chopped fresh dill

salt

coarse ground black pepper

Combine all ingredients in small mixing bowl. Refrigerate until ready to use.

Tarragon Mayonnaise

By simply combining prepared mayonnaise with herbs, an entirely new flavor is introduced to sandwich making. I encourage you to experiment with herbs, spices, and flavorings to create your own favorite spreads and mayonnaises for use on any sandwich, panini, or wrap.

½ cup (112 g) mayonnaise

1 tablespoon (14 g) sour cream

2 tablespoons (8 g) chopped, fresh tarragon

½ teaspoon (2.5 ml) tarragon vinegar (optional)

Place all ingredients in a small mixing bowl and stir to combine. Cover and refrigerate for at least 30 minutes.

[Makes about ½ cup (120 ml)]

Grilled Onion Relish

Much like caramelizing onions, grilling onions intensifies the natural sweetness hiding within those skins. If you prefer Vidalia onions or another variety to red onions, feel free to substitute. This relish will enhance a variety of other dishes, such as grilled fish, meats, and poultry.

1 large red onion, thinly sliced

2 tablespoons (30 ml) olive oil

1 tablespoon (15 ml) red wine vinegar

½ teaspoon (.5 g) chopped fresh oregano

coarse ground black pepper

Combine vinegar and oregano in small bowl. Preheat outdoor grill or stovetop grill pan to medium-high. Coat onion slices with olive oil and season with pepper. Grill until browned and tender, about 7 minutes per side. Transfer from grill to cutting board and let cool. When cool enough to handle, cut rings in half and combine with vinegar and oregano. Use immediately or cover and refrigerate up to 5 days.

[Makes about ½ cup (112 g)]

Spicy Tartar Sauce

¼ cup (60 g) sour cream

¼ cup (55 g) mayonnaise

2 teaspoons (5 g) grated lemon rind

1 tablespoon (4 g) chopped fresh italian flat-leaf parsley

1 tablespoon (8 g) minced green onion

1 tablespoon (8 g) minced red onion

1 teaspoon (5 ml) fresh lemon juice

¼ teaspoon (1.3 ml) hot sauce

Combine all the ingredients in a small bowl. Use immediately or cover and refrigerate up to 7 days.

3 cloves Roasted Garlic (see recipe, page 29), garlic squeezed out of cloves

½ teaspoon (3 g) salt

1 large egg yolk

1 teaspoon (5 g) Dijon mustard

1 cup (235 ml) extra-virgin olive oil

1 teaspoon (5 ml) lemon juice

½ teaspoon (1 g) coarse ground black pepper

Combine roasted garlic with the salt, then mash the two together using the back of a spoon to make a paste. Whisk in egg yolk and Dijon mustard. While whisking, gradually add the olive oil in a steady stream to emulsify. The mixture will become thick, white, and creamy like mayonnaise. Continue adding the oil until a thick, creamy emulsion forms. Add lemon juice and black pepper and combine. Cover and refrigerate until ready for use. If adding flavorings or herbs, incorporate them before use.

[Makes about 2 cups (475 ml)]

Roasted Garlic Aioli

Making your own aioli (mayonnaise) is simple and rewarding. The beauty of making your own aioli is that once you've mastered the recipe, you can add any combination of flavors and herbs for endless variations.

Whole-Grain Molasses Mustard

There are numerous mustards available in your grocery and specialty food stores, but making your own allows you to control the flavor intensity. The sweetness of molasses is perfect with the bitterness of whole-grain mustard.

³/₄ cup (180 g) whole-grain mustard

1 tablespoon (14 g) butter, room temperature

1 tablespoon (20 g) honey

1 tablespoon (20 g) molasses

1 tablespoon (6 g) fresh chopped chives

Combine mustard and butter in a small bowl, then blend with a fork until well mixed. Add honey, molasses, and chives, and stir to combine. Set aside or refrigerate until ready to use.

[Makes about ½ cup (120 ml)]

Herbed Feta Spread

Feta cheese is a good base for an array of herbs, but any other soft, dry cheese may be used instead. Vary this recipe according to your own taste preferences. As with many of my recipes for condiments and spreads, the combination of ingredients is a suggestion—the recipe can be altered to suit your own tastes and culinary creativity.

¼ cup (28 g) cream cheese, room temperature

¼ cup (55 g) sour cream

4 ounces (115 g) feta cheese, room temperature

1 teaspoon (5 ml) fresh lemon juice

6 leaves fresh basil, minced

1 tablespoon (6 g) chopped fresh chives

¼ teaspoon (.3 g) dried oregano

¼ teaspoon (1.5 g) salt

¼ teaspoon (.5 g) coarse ground black pepper

Combine all ingredients in a bowl and mash together using a fork until well mixed. Cover and refrigerate until ready to use.

chapter 5

Dessert—**Pairing the Sweet and the Savory**

I believe that every good meal, whether eaten on the go or not, should finish with a sweet treat. In keeping with the mobility of the sandwich, these desserts are easy to prepare ahead of time, and they pack and travel easily.

1½ cup (165 g) all-purpose flour

2 teaspoons (3 g) baking powder

½ teaspoon (3 g) salt

PUDDING:

4 ounces (115 g) unsweetened chocolate

¾ cup (170 g) firmly packed brown sugar

1½ cups (355 ml) heavy cream, warmed

2 large eggs

1 teaspoon (5 ml) pure vanilla extract

½ lb (225 g) unsalted butter, melted

6 ounces (170 g) semisweet chocolate, chopped into ¼" (0.6 cm)-chunks

PECAN CRUMBLE:

1 cup (125 g) pecans

¼ cup (55 g) firmly packed brown sugar

¼ cup (28 g) all-purpose flour

1 teaspoon (2.6 g) ground cinnamon

¼ teaspoon (1.5 g) salt

3 tablespoons (45 g) chilled unsalted butter, cut into chunks

1½ cups (355 ml) Kahlua Sauce (recipe follows)

KAHLUA SAUCE:

Makes 1½ cups (355 ml)

6 tablespoons (90 g) unsalted butter

1 cup (235 ml) Kahlúa or other coffee-flavored liqueur

½ cup (120 g) granulated sugar

1 egg

Preheat oven to 350°F (175°C). Sift together flour, baking powder, and salt, and set aside. Place pecans in a single layer on a baking dish. Position on center rack of oven and toast for about 10 minutes. Remove from oven, allow to cool, and chop. Transfer chopped pecans to a bowl, and add brown sugar, flour, cinnamon, salt, and butter. Combine ingredients with your fingers until you achieve a crumbly texture, then set aside.

Place a nonreactive stainless steel or glass bowl over a saucepan of boiling water, add chocolate, and melt, stirring constantly. Add brown sugar and stir to dissolve. Add heavy cream and stir to combine. Once heavy cream is incorporated and the chocolate is smooth and melted, remove from heat and set aside.

Whisk together eggs, vanilla extract, and melted butter in a large mixing bowl; whisk until well combined. Add the melted chocolate to the egg mixture in a slow, steady stream, whisking constantly. Once the chocolate and egg mixture are thoroughly combined, add the dry ingredients by folding them in using a rubber spatula. Scrape the sides and bottom of the bowl to thoroughly mix the wet and dry ingredients. Add the chocolate chunks and stir to incorporate. Pour batter into a greased 9-inch (23 cm) square baking dish. Top evenly with pecan crumble. Position on middle rack of oven and bake for 45 minutes or until a wooden skewer inserted in the center comes out clean. Cut into squares and serve topped with Kahlua Sauce.

[Makes 24 brownies]

Chewy Chocolate Chunk Brownies with Pecan Crumble and Kahlúa Drizzle

These brownies may become the new favorite in your house. The batter is moist and chewy, and the finished brownies will surprise you with the sugary crunch of pecan crumble and huge chunks of chocolate throughout.

[For Kahlúa sauce]

Melt the butter in a small saucepan over medium heat. Add Kahlúa and sugar, and stir to dissolve the sugar. Bring the mixture to a boil, then remove from heat. In a small bowl, whisk the egg lightly, then gradually whisk the warm Kahlúa mixture into the egg 1 tablespoon (15 ml) at a time. After you have whisked about 4 tablespoons (60 ml) of Kahlúa mixture with the egg, add the egg mixture to the saucepan of Kahlúa sauce. Return saucepan to low heat, whisking constantly, to incorporate the egg, then cook for 2 minutes. Remove from heat and set aside until ready to use. Serve warm. Sauce can be sealed in a tight container and refrigerated for up to 1 week.

2 sticks (½ lb [225 g]) margarine

1 cup (150 g) brown sugar

1 cup (120 g) sugar

2 eggs

2 cups (220 g) all-purpose flour

1 teaspoon (1.5 g) baking soda

½ teaspoon (0.75 g) baking powder

½ teaspoon (3 g) salt

1 teaspoon (2.5 g) cinnamon

2 cups (150 g) rolled oats

1 (6-ounce [170 g]) package semisweet chocolate chips

1 teaspoon (5 ml) vanilla extract

Preheat oven to 350°F (175°C). Cream margarine and sugars in a large mixing bowl. Add eggs and mix well. Add dry ingredients (except oatmeal) and mix well. Stir in oatmeal and vanilla extract. Gently fold in chocolate chips. Using a small ice cream scoop to shape cookies, drop them onto a nonstick baking sheet about 2 inches (5 cm) apart. Bake for 8 minutes. Remove from oven and let cool on sheet pan. Serve.

[Makes 24 cookies]

Colossal Chocolate Chip Oatmeal Cookies (a.k.a. "Tweety Cookies")

From the famed Camp Mystic in Hunt, Texas, my dear friend Tweety Eastland developed these cookies years ago to offer to her young campers as a special treat. After working at camp Mystic for five years, I decided these chewy, crunchy, moist, and delicious cookies needed to be a staple in my recipe box.

[Makes about 2 dozen squares]

Chocolate Caramel Rice Cereal Bars

My version of this classic combination uses chocolate and caramel for a gooey—but delicious—mess of a dessert.

4 tablespoons (60 g) butter, divided

1 (10.5-ounce [295 g]) bag large or small marshmallows

¼ cup (60 ml) light corn syrup

7 cups (1,330 g) crisp rice cereal

½ cup (90 g) semisweet chocolate morsels or chunks

CARAMEL DRIZZLE:

10 cubes individually wrapped caramel candies, unwrapped

1 teaspoon (5 ml) water

CHOCOLATE DRIZZLE:

6 ounces (170 g) semisweet chocolate, chopped

3 tablespoons (45 ml) heavy cream

1 tablespoon (14 g) butter

In a large nonstick pan, melt 3 tablespoons (45 g) butter over medium heat. Add the marshmallows and corn syrup, and stir until marshmallows are completely melted. Add rice cereal and ½ cup (90 g) of the chocolate chunks; stir to combine. Spread evenly in a greased 9" × 13" × 2" (23 × 33 × 5 cm) pan. Set aside to harden.

In the top of a double boiler set over hot water, melt the chocolate, stirring occasionally. Add the cream and butter and stir until smooth. In a small, microwave-safe bowl, heat the caramel and water in the microwave for 2 minutes on high until the caramel is melted. Remove and stir vigorously to combine. Drizzle chocolate sauce and caramel sauce over the bars, let stand until firm, cut into squares, and serve.

Luscious Lemon Bars

A picnic or lunch buffet just isn't complete
without the tangy, tender bite of a lemon bar.

CRUST:

2 cups (200 g) gingersnap crumbs

2 tablespoons (30 g)
granulated sugar

7 tablespoons (100 g)
unsalted butter, melted

FILLING:

6 eggs

2 cups (480 g) sugar

1/3 cup (35 g) all-purpose flour

1/4 teaspoon (1.5 g) salt

3 tablespoons (15 g) lemon zest

3/4 cup (175 ml) milk

Preheat oven to 350°F (175°C). Combine all crust ingredients and press into the bottom and one-quarter way up the sides of a 9" × 13" (23 × 33 cm) baking dish. Bake until golden and crisp, about 8 to 10 minutes. Remove from oven and let cool. Reduce oven to 325°F (160°C). Whisk eggs, then add sugar, flour, and salt, and stir to combine. Mix in lemon zest and milk. Pour over prebaked crust and bake 20 minutes more until set. Chill for 2 hours before cutting. Dust with powdered sugar and serve.

Key Lime Shortbread Bars

Key lime pie is such a unique and flavorful dessert; I made it into a more portable version, with a lovely shortbread crust.

CRUST:

1½ sticks (¾ cup [170 g]) unsalted butter

2 cups (220 g) all-purpose flour

½ cup (112 g) packed light brown sugar

½ teaspoon (3 g) salt

¼ teaspoon (.5 g) cinnamon

¼ cup (30 g) finely chopped almonds

FILLING:

1 large egg

4 large egg yolks

2 (14.5-ounce [411 g]) cans unsweetened condensed milk

½ cup (120 ml) bottled key lime juice

½ cup (120 ml) coconut milk

¼ cup (18 g) toasted coconut flakes

¼ teaspoon (1.3 ml) almond extract

Preheat oven to 350°F (175°C). Cut the butter into small chunks. Place all the crust ingredients into the bowl of a food processor fitted with the blade attachment and process until crumbly and small lumps form. Sprinkle mixture into a 9" × 13" (23 × 33 cm) baking pan, then press evenly onto bottom. Bake crust on the middle rack until golden, about 20 minutes. Remove and let cool. Reduce oven temperature to 325°F (165°C). For the filling, whisk together egg and yolks in a large mixing bowl, then add condensed milk and combine. Add the lime juice, coconut milk, and extract and combine thoroughly. Fold in coconut. Pour mixture evenly over the prebaked shortbread crust. Bake until the filling is set, about 20 minutes. Cool the bars completely in the pan. Refrigerate for at least 2 hours, then cut into bars and serve.

[Makes about 24 dessert cups]

S'mores Cups

This recipe makes a campfire classic portable.

CRUST:

2 cups (200 g) graham
cracker crumbs

2 tablespoons (30 g)
granulated sugar

7 tablespoons (100 g)
unsalted butter, melted

FILLING:

6 ounces (170 g)
semisweet chocolate

3 tablespoons (45 ml) heavy cream

1 tablespoon (14 g) butter

1½ cups (320 23g)
Fluff marshmallow product

Preheat oven to 350°F (175°C). Combine all crust ingredients in a bowl and mix until crumbly. Press the crust mixture onto the bottom and up the sides of 24 cups of a minimuffin tin. Bake for 8 to 10 minutes, remove from oven, and let cool. In the top of a double boiler set over high heat, melt the chocolate, then add the cream and butter and stir to combine. Coat the bottom of each baked graham cracker cup with chocolate sauce, then cover and refrigerate until set, about 30 minutes. Preheat broiler to high. Remove tins from refrigerator and place a heaping spoonful of Fluff marshmallow product in each cup. Brown marshmallow topping under broiler until golden, then serve warm.

Toffee Candy Crumble

This treat is very easy to prepare and a great on-the-go sweet.

1 cup (225 g) butter (not margarine), plus extra for coating pan

---

1 cup (240 g) sugar

---

1 tablespoon (15 ml) light corn syrup

---

3 tablespoons (45 ml) water

---

4 (6-ounce [170 g]) chocolate bars, preferably Hershey, broken into large pieces

---

$^{1}/_{2}$ cup (60 g) sliced almonds, toasted

Butter a 10" × 15" (25 × 38 cm) cookie sheet. Melt 1 cup (225 g) butter with sugar, corn syrup, and water in a medium saucepan. Bring to boil and cook on medium until the mixture reaches the hard-crack stage on a candy thermometer (325°F (165°C)), taking care not to allow the syrup to brown. Pour the syrup mixture onto the cookie sheet, and maneuver the pan back and forth with your hands to spread the syrup evenly over the pan. Immediately top with broken chocolate bars, placing pieces randomly over syrup mixture (the heat of the syrup will melt the bars.) Once the chocolate pieces have melted, spread the chocolate evenly using a rubber spatula. Sprinkle with toasted almonds. Refrigerate uncovered for about 15 minutes or until candy is set and chocolate is hardened. Remove, break into random pieces, and serve. Candy can be refrigerated in airtight bags for up to 1 week.

Index

Acknowledgments

The books that I have written have been labor intensive for not only myself but for many behind the scenes. I thank first Rockport Publishers and Quarry Books, who have given me the chance to share my cooking with everyone through what are truly beautiful compositions. Thank you, once again, to my friend Silke Braun, art director and stylist, and of course, to my friend Allen Penn for his beautiful photography. I have realized, through proofreading ample pages of my own text, that I could be an editor's nightmare! Thank you to all of you who lend an eye to correcting my mistakes in copy. I truly appreciate the time, effort, and energy that everyone contributes to the production of these books. Thank you so much to both Winnie Prentice and Rochelle Bourgault for their editorial direction on these projects. Their patience and creative eye are much appreciated. In addition to those who are responsible for getting a book to print, I thank my friends and family for their critiques and input on my writing. No one author or food writer can concoct enough of a feast to fill the pages on his or her own. Recipe developing is a thought-intensive process that is the product of many suggestions and ideas. I have to acknowledge the two girls that keep me company through the long hours of recipe developing and testing and the extensive days at my computer typing and writing—Bailey and Bongo, my two beloved dogs!

Lastly and once again I offer a huge thanks to those of you that support my efforts by purchasing my books. I truly enjoy sharing my recipes and thoughts with you, and hope that I inspire you to cook creatively along the way.

About the Author

Dwayne Ridgaway, although a native of Kerrville, Texas, now lives in Bristol, Rhode Island. He is the author of Lasagna: **The Art of Layered Cooking** and **Pizza: 50 Traditional and Alternative Recipes for the Oven and Grill**, and a contributing writer, food stylist, and recipe developer for several cooking magazines. Dwayne currently works in Rhode Island as a food and beverage consultant, caterer, and event designer. A graduate of the highly respected Johnson and Wales University, Dwayne has made a career out of exploring and celebrating the culinary arts. His passions lie in fresh ingredients and new flavors. Exploring everything the world has to offer in both techniques and flavors, Dwayne makes it his goal to combine these elements with inspired cooking to develop recipes that anyone can execute and enjoy. With **Sandwiches, Panini, and Wraps**, Dwayne hopes home cooks everywhere will begin to explore their tastes and passions and use his recipes and writing as groundwork for their own personal creativity.